THIS BOOK BELONGS TO

_____

_____

_____

LILLIAN DAVID

CONNECTIONS PUZZLES BOOK

CONSERVATION	BASENJI	WELCOME	RETRIEVER
PEDDLE	HOUND	WETLAND	DEFORESTATION
MASTIFF	HEAVENLY	OPEL	ROBUST
AUTO	AUTOMOTIVE	FINE	ENVIRONMENT

**A challenging game to generate
four groups of four words
that share something in common.**

Contents

4

HOW TO PLAY

INSTRUCTIONS:

1. Look at the words and read them well.

LENTILS	HIPPOPOTAMUS	ROAMING	MULBERRY
CROSSING	BLUEBERRY	EXCURSION	VOYAGE
LOGANBERRY	FENNEL	HUCKLEBERRY	CHEETAH
SUPPER	ZEBRA	RHINO	PERSIMMON

Within each game, there exists a set of precisely 16 words that require identification of a "hidden relationship." The ultimate objective of this exercise is to adeptly categorize the words into four distinct groups.

2. Identify the four words that can be connected

HIPPOPOTAMUS

CHEETAH

ZEBRA   RHINO

3. Extract the other three categories

Choose four words that you believe could potentially share a meaningful correlation.

Mammals : Zebra, Rhino, Hippopotamus, Cheetah

Mammals : Zebra, Rhino, Hippopotamus, Cheetah

Fruit : Huckleberry, Loganberry, Mulberry, Persimmon

Food : Fennel, Blueberry, Supper, Lentils

Journey : Roaming, Voyage, Excursion, Crossing

✔ Sometimes there are words that could fit into two different categories.

Puzzle # 1

The solution is on page # 207

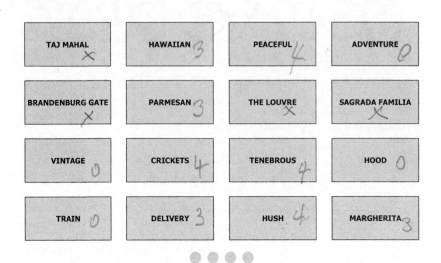

TAJ MAHAL ✗	HAWAIIAN 3	PEACEFUL 4	ADVENTURE 0
BRANDENBURG GATE ✗	PARMESAN 3	THE LOUVRE ✗	SAGRADA FAMILIA ✗
VINTAGE 0	CRICKETS 4	TENEBROUS 4	HOOD 0
TRAIN 0	DELIVERY 3	HUSH 4	MARGHERITA 3

● ● ● ●

Four groups of four words that share something in common :

Group #1 : _____

_____ _____ _____ _____

Group #2 : _____

_____ _____ _____ _____

Group #3 : _____

_____ _____ _____ _____

Group #4 : _____

_____ _____ _____ _____

Puzzle # 2

The solution is on page # 207

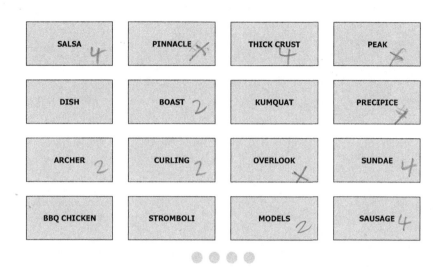

SALSA 4	PINNACLE ✗	THICK CRUST 4	PEAK ✗
DISH	BOAST 2	KUMQUAT	PRECIPICE ✗
ARCHER 2	CURLING 2	OVERLOOK ✗	SUNDAE 4
BBQ CHICKEN	STROMBOLI	MODELS 2	SAUSAGE 4

Four groups of four words that share something in common :

Group #1 : _____

_____   _____   _____   _____

Group #2 : _____

_____   _____   _____   _____

Group #3 : _____

_____   _____   _____   _____

Group #4 : _____

_____   _____   _____   _____

Puzzle # 3

The solution is on page # 207

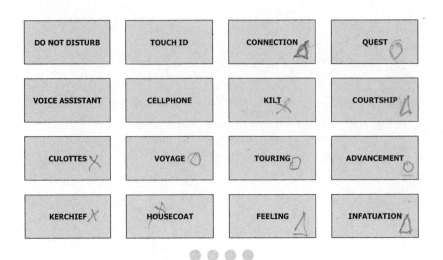

Four groups of four words that share something in common :

Group #1 : _____

_____ _____ _____ _____

Group #2 : _____

_____ _____ _____ _____

Group #3 : _____

_____ _____ _____ _____

Group #4 : _____

_____ _____ _____ _____

Puzzle # 4

The solution is on page # 207

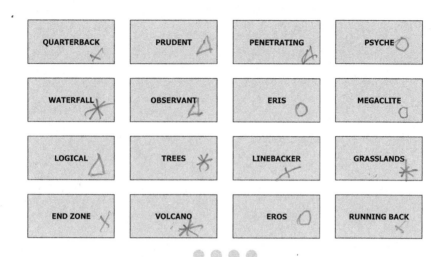

Four groups of four words that share something in common :

Group #1 : _____

_____ _____ _____ _____

Group #2 : _____

_____ _____ _____ _____

Group #3 : _____

_____ _____ _____ _____

Group #4 : _____

_____ _____ _____ _____

9

Puzzle # 5

The solution is on page # 207

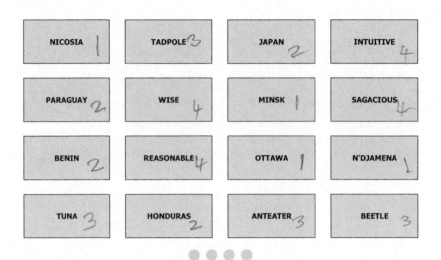

NICOSIA 1

TADPOLE 3

JAPAN 2

INTUITIVE 4

PARAGUAY 2

WISE 4

MINSK 1

SAGACIOUS 4

BENIN 2

REASONABLE 4

OTTAWA 1

N'DJAMENA 1

TUNA 3

HONDURAS 2

ANTEATER 3

BEETLE 3

Four groups of four words that share something in common :

Group #1 : _____

_____ _____ _____ _____

Group #2 : _____

_____ _____ _____ _____

Group #3 : _____

_____ _____ _____ _____

Group #4 : _____

_____ _____ _____ _____

Puzzle # 6

The solution is on page # 208

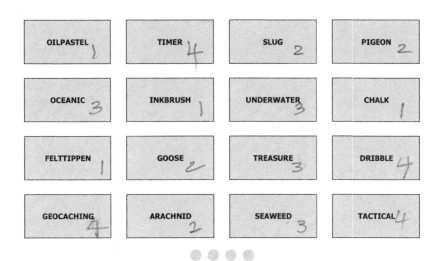

OILPASTEL *2*	TIMER *4*	SLUG *2*	PIGEON *2*
OCEANIC *3*	INKBRUSH *1*	UNDERWATER *3*	CHALK *1*
FELTTIPPEN *1*	GOOSE *2*	TREASURE *3*	DRIBBLE *4*
GEOCACHING *4*	ARACHNID *2*	SEAWEED *3*	TACTICAL *4*

Four groups of four words that share something in common :

Group #1 : _____

_____ _____ _____ _____

Group #2 : _____

_____ _____ _____ _____

Group #3 : _____

_____ _____ _____ _____

Group #4 : _____

_____ _____ _____ _____

Puzzle # 7

The solution is on page # 208

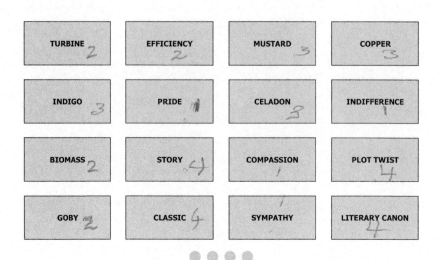

TURBINE _2_	EFFICIENCY _2_	MUSTARD _3_	COPPER _3_
INDIGO _3_	PRIDE	CELADON _3_	INDIFFERENCE _1_
BIOMASS _2_	STORY _4_	COMPASSION _1_	PLOT TWIST _4_
GOBY _2_	CLASSIC _4_	SYMPATHY	LITERARY CANON _4_

Four groups of four words that share something in common :

Group #1 : _____

_____ _____ _____ _____

Group #2 : _____

_____ _____ _____ _____

Group #3 : _____

_____ _____ _____ _____

Group #4 : _____

_____ _____ _____ _____

Puzzle # 8

The solution is on page # 208

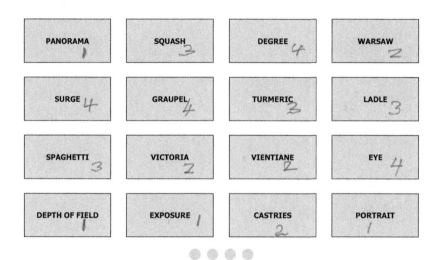

PANORAMA *1*	SQUASH *3*	DEGREE *4*	WARSAW *2*
SURGE *4*	GRAUPEL *4*	TURMERIC *3*	LADLE *3*
SPAGHETTI *3*	VICTORIA *2*	VIENTIANE *2*	EYE *4*
DEPTH OF FIELD *1*	EXPOSURE *1*	CASTRIES *2*	PORTRAIT *1*

● ● ● ●

Four groups of four words that share something in common :

Group #1 : _____

_____ _____ _____ _____

Group #2 : _____

_____ _____ _____ _____

Group #3 : _____

_____ _____ _____ _____

Group #4 : _____

_____ _____ _____ _____

13

Puzzle # 9

The solution is on page # 208

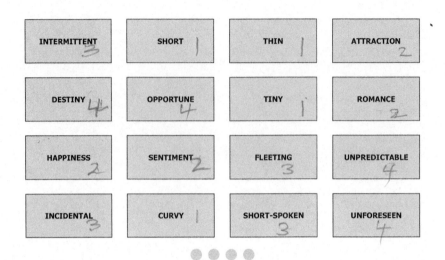

INTERMITTENT 3	SHORT	THIN	ATTRACTION 2
DESTINY 4	OPPORTUNE 4	TINY	ROMANCE 2
HAPPINESS 2	SENTIMENT 2	FLEETING 3	UNPREDICTABLE 4
INCIDENTAL 3	CURVY	SHORT-SPOKEN 3	UNFORESEEN 4

Four groups of four words that share something in common :

Group #1 : _____

_____   _____   _____   _____

Group #2 : _____

_____   _____   _____   _____

Group #3 : _____

_____   _____   _____   _____

Group #4 : _____

_____   _____   _____   _____

Puzzle # 10

The solution is on page # 208

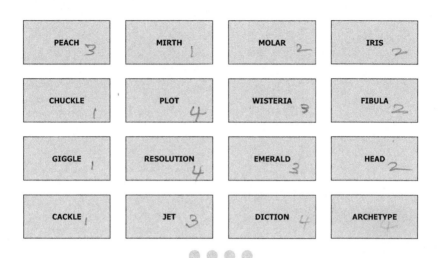

PEACH 3	MIRTH 1	MOLAR 2	IRIS 2
CHUCKLE 1	PLOT 4	WISTERIA 3	FIBULA 2
GIGGLE 1	RESOLUTION 4	EMERALD 3	HEAD 2
CACKLE 1	JET 3	DICTION 4	ARCHETYPE 4

Four groups of four words that share something in common :

Group #1 : _____

_____ _____ _____ _____

Group #2 : _____

_____ _____ _____ _____

Group #3 : _____

_____ _____ _____ _____

Group #4 : _____

_____ _____ _____ _____

15

Puzzle # 11

The solution is on page # 209

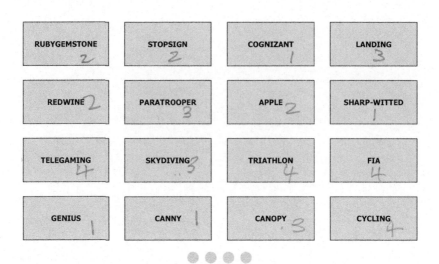

RUBYGEMSTONE *2*	STOPSIGN *2*	COGNIZANT *1*	LANDING *3*
REDWINE *2*	PARATROOPER *3*	APPLE *2*	SHARP-WITTED *1*
TELEGAMING *4*	SKYDIVING *3*	TRIATHLON *4*	FIA *4*
GENIUS *1*	CANNY *1*	CANOPY *3*	CYCLING *4*

Four groups of four words that share something in common :

Group #1 : _____

_____   _____   _____   _____

Group #2 : _____

_____   _____   _____   _____

Group #3 : _____

_____   _____   _____   _____

Group #4 : _____

_____   _____   _____   _____

Puzzle # 12

The solution is on page # 209

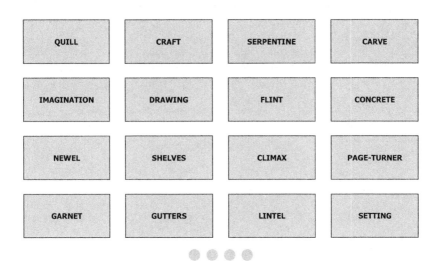

Four groups of four words that share something in common :

Group #1 : _____

_____ _____ _____ _____

Group #2 : _____

_____ _____ _____ _____

Group #3 : _____

_____ _____ _____ _____

Group #4 : _____

_____ _____ _____ _____

Puzzle # 13

The solution is on page # 209

Four groups of four words that share something in common :

Group #1 : _____

_____ _____ _____ _____

Group #2 : _____

_____ _____ _____ _____

Group #3 : _____

_____ _____ _____ _____

Group #4 : _____

_____ _____ _____ _____

Puzzle # 14

The solution is on page # 209

TAKEOUT	CONFUSION	FOG	DEEP-DISH
JUDICIOUS	SUBMARINE	CLEAR-SIGHTED	MUSHROOM
DISTORT	ASTUTE	INFORMED	CANOE
BRICK OVEN	YACHT	CRUISESHIP	PERPLEXITY

Four groups of four words that share something in common :

Group #1 : _____

_____ _____ _____ _____

Group #2 : _____

_____ _____ _____ _____

Group #3 : _____

_____ _____ _____ _____

Group #4 : _____

_____ _____ _____ _____

Puzzle # 15

The solution is on page # 209

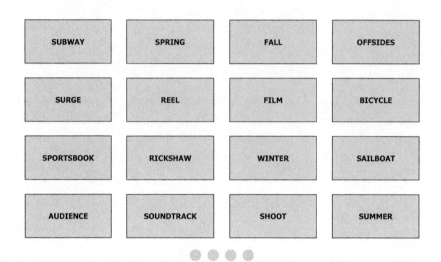

Four groups of four words that share something in common :

Group #1 : _____

_____ _____ _____ _____

Group #2 : _____

_____ _____ _____ _____

Group #3 : _____

_____ _____ _____ _____

Group #4 : _____

_____ _____ _____ _____

Puzzle # 16

The solution is on page # 210

HOOT	SAGACIOUS	ALL-PERMEATING	PARSNIP
STARS	CLOUD	IMMANENT	SKY
KOWTOW	MYSTIFICATION	ASPARAGUS	CANDLELIGHT
EVERLASTING	INESCAPABLE	DRESSING	FRUIT

● ● ● ●

Four groups of four words that share something in common :

Group #1 : _____

_____ _____ _____ _____

Group #2 : _____

_____ _____ _____ _____

Group #3 : _____

_____ _____ _____ _____

Group #4 : _____

_____ _____ _____ _____

Puzzle # 17

The solution is on page # 210

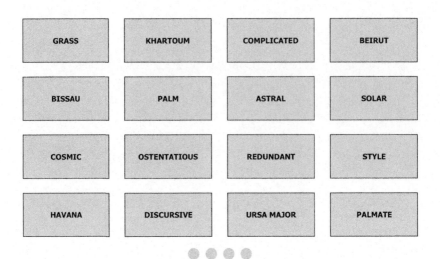

GRASS	KHARTOUM	COMPLICATED	BEIRUT
BISSAU	PALM	ASTRAL	SOLAR
COSMIC	OSTENTATIOUS	REDUNDANT	STYLE
HAVANA	DISCURSIVE	URSA MAJOR	PALMATE

Four groups of four words that share something in common :

Group #1 : _____

_____   _____   _____   _____

Group #2 : _____

_____   _____   _____   _____

Group #3 : _____

_____   _____   _____   _____

Group #4 : _____

_____   _____   _____   _____

Puzzle # 18

The solution is on page # 210

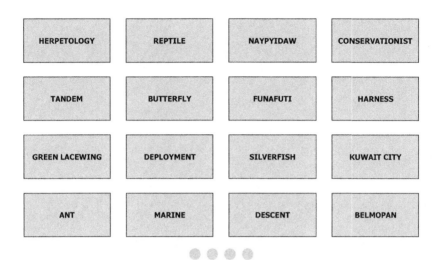

HERPETOLOGY	REPTILE	NAYPYIDAW	CONSERVATIONIST
TANDEM	BUTTERFLY	FUNAFUTI	HARNESS
GREEN LACEWING	DEPLOYMENT	SILVERFISH	KUWAIT CITY
ANT	MARINE	DESCENT	BELMOPAN

Four groups of four words that share something in common :

Group #1 : _____

_____ _____ _____ _____

Group #2 : _____

_____ _____ _____ _____

Group #3 : _____

_____ _____ _____ _____

Group #4 : _____

_____ _____ _____ _____

Puzzle # 19

The solution is on page # 210

Four groups of four words that share something in common :

Group #1 : _____

_____   _____   _____   _____

Group #2 : _____

_____   _____   _____   _____

Group #3 : _____

_____   _____   _____   _____

Group #4 : _____

_____   _____   _____   _____

Puzzle # 20

The solution is on page # 210

MERRY	LONDON	EBULLIENT	COMMUNICATION
NAIROBI	TECH ECOSYSTEM	ADVANCEMENT	ASUNCIÓN
TECH INDUSTRY	BAKU	IRREPRESSIBLE	TRAFFIC
JUBILANT	GEOMETRY	THEOREM	PENROSE

Four groups of four words that share something in common :

Group #1 : _____

_____   _____   _____   _____

Group #2 : _____

_____   _____   _____   _____

Group #3 : _____

_____   _____   _____   _____

Group #4 : _____

_____   _____   _____   _____

Puzzle # 21

The solution is on page # 211

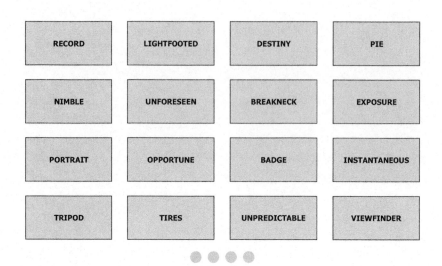

Four groups of four words that share something in common :

Group #1 : _____

_____ _____ _____ _____

Group #2 : _____

_____ _____ _____ _____

Group #3 : _____

_____ _____ _____ _____

Group #4 : _____

_____ _____ _____ _____

Puzzle # 22

The solution is on page # 211

AUGUST	AFTERNOON	RECIPE	SETTING
RICE	PAGE-TURNER	SEINEN	NEWYEARSDAY
DRAMA	NIGHT	MECHA	IMAGINATION
SAMURAI	MUNCH	CASSAVA	CLIMAX

● ● ● ●

Four groups of four words that share something in common :

Group #1 : _____

_____ _____ _____ _____

Group #2 : _____

_____ _____ _____ _____

Group #3 : _____

_____ _____ _____ _____

Group #4 : _____

_____ _____ _____ _____

Puzzle # 23

The solution is on page # 211

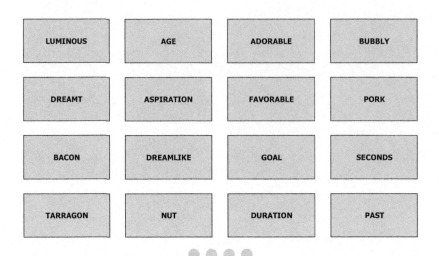

LUMINOUS	AGE	ADORABLE	BUBBLY
DREAMT	ASPIRATION	FAVORABLE	PORK
BACON	DREAMLIKE	GOAL	SECONDS
TARRAGON	NUT	DURATION	PAST

Four groups of four words that share something in common :

Group #1 : _____

_____   _____   _____   _____

Group #2 : _____

_____   _____   _____   _____

Group #3 : _____

_____   _____   _____   _____

Group #4 : _____

_____   _____   _____   _____

Puzzle # 24

The solution is on page # 211

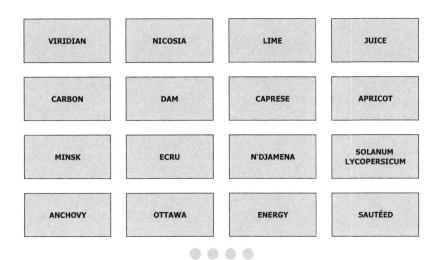

Four groups of four words that share something in common :

Group #1 : _____

_____ _____ _____ _____

Group #2 : _____

_____ _____ _____ _____

Group #3 : _____

_____ _____ _____ _____

Group #4 : _____

_____ _____ _____ _____

Puzzle # 25

The solution is on page # 211

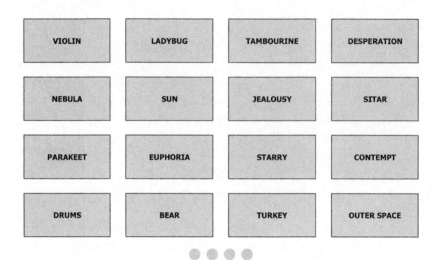

Four groups of four words that share something in common :

Group #1 : _____

_____ _____ _____ _____

Group #2 : _____

_____ _____ _____ _____

Group #3 : _____

_____ _____ _____ _____

Group #4 : _____

_____ _____ _____ _____

Puzzle # 26

The solution is on page # 212

COMET	WANING	BRUSH	HALIBUT
ICEFISH	INK	MALLETS	WALLEYE
ARIOSO	CORONA	RADIANT	TONIC
FORTE	DECORATE	PERCH	CONTRAST

Four groups of four words that share something in common :

Group #1 : _____

_____ _____ _____ _____

Group #2 : _____

_____ _____ _____ _____

Group #3 : _____

_____ _____ _____ _____

Group #4 : _____

_____ _____ _____ _____

Puzzle # 27

The solution is on page # 212

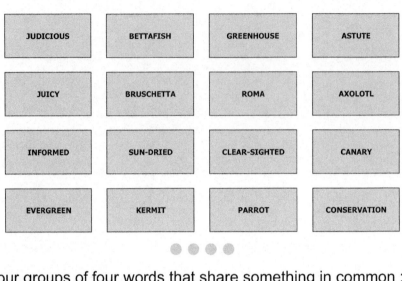

JUDICIOUS	BETTAFISH	GREENHOUSE	ASTUTE
JUICY	BRUSCHETTA	ROMA	AXOLOTL
INFORMED	SUN-DRIED	CLEAR-SIGHTED	CANARY
EVERGREEN	KERMIT	PARROT	CONSERVATION

Four groups of four words that share something in common :

Group #1 : _____

_____ _____ _____ _____

Group #2 : _____

_____ _____ _____ _____

Group #3 : _____

_____ _____ _____ _____

Group #4 : _____

_____ _____ _____ _____

Puzzle # 28

The solution is on page # 212

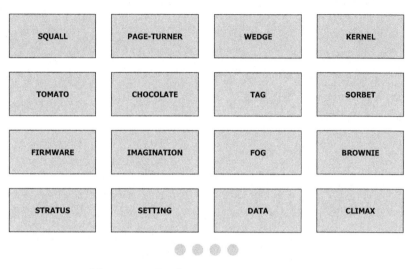

Four groups of four words that share something in common :

Group #1 : _____

_____ _____ _____ _____

Group #2 : _____

_____ _____ _____ _____

Group #3 : _____

_____ _____ _____ _____

Group #4 : _____

_____ _____ _____ _____

Puzzle # 29

The solution is on page # 212

NURTURING	AUSTRIA	CREW	SPAR
CASUAL	CREATIVE	POPULAR	GRAVE
CYMBALS	DEFENCE	POLAND	CONSTANT
SCHERZO	CONCH	LIBERIA	BELIZE

Four groups of four words that share something in common :

Group #1 : _____

_____ _____ _____ _____

Group #2 : _____

_____ _____ _____ _____

Group #3 : _____

_____ _____ _____ _____

Group #4 : _____

_____ _____ _____ _____

Puzzle # 30

The solution is on page # 212

LOVELY   TRAIPSE   PLOD   REPTILE

BRILLIANT   THANKSGIVING   NEW YEAR'S   CONSERVATIONIST

HALLOWEEN   WHOLESOME   CHRISTMAS   CHAMP

HERPETOLOGY   MARINE   PROMENADE   LURCH

Four groups of four words that share something in common :

Group #1 : _____

_____ _____ _____ _____

Group #2 : _____

_____ _____ _____ _____

Group #3 : _____

_____ _____ _____ _____

Group #4 : _____

_____ _____ _____ _____

Puzzle # 31

The solution is on page # 213

Four groups of four words that share something in common :

Group #1 : _____

_____ _____ _____ _____

Group #2 : _____

_____ _____ _____ _____

Group #3 : _____

_____ _____ _____ _____

Group #4 : _____

_____ _____ _____ _____

Puzzle # 32

The solution is on page # 213

PUMICE	PIRATE	BISON	BASENJI
MARBLE	RETRIEVER	ALUMINA	MASTIFF
SURF	MANTIS	LIGHTHOUSE	IMPALA
BEACHCOMBING	METEORITE	WHELK	HOUND

● ● ● ●

Four groups of four words that share something in common :

Group #1 : _____

_____ _____ _____ _____

Group #2 : _____

_____ _____ _____ _____

Group #3 : _____

_____ _____ _____ _____

Group #4 : _____

_____ _____ _____ _____

Puzzle # 33

The solution is on page # 213

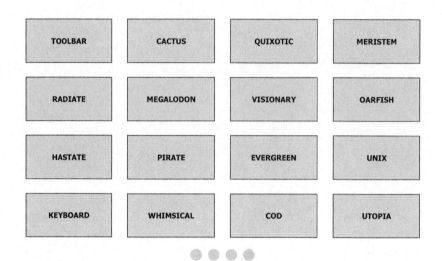

Four groups of four words that share something in common :

Group #1 : _____

_____ _____ _____ _____

Group #2 : _____

_____ _____ _____ _____

Group #3 : _____

_____ _____ _____ _____

Group #4 : _____

_____ _____ _____ _____

Puzzle # 34

The solution is on page # 213

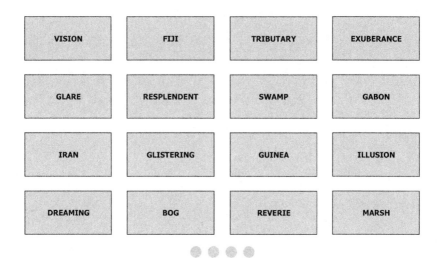

Four groups of four words that share something in common :

Group #1 : _____

_____   _____   _____   _____

Group #2 : _____

_____   _____   _____   _____

Group #3 : _____

_____   _____   _____   _____

Group #4 : _____

_____   _____   _____   _____

Puzzle # 35

The solution is on page # 213

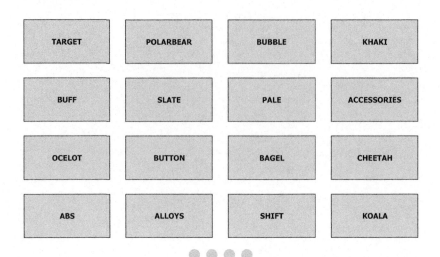

Four groups of four words that share something in common :

Group #1 : _____

_____ _____ _____ _____

Group #2 : _____

_____ _____ _____ _____

Group #3 : _____

_____ _____ _____ _____

Group #4 : _____

_____ _____ _____ _____

Puzzle # 36

The solution is on page # 214

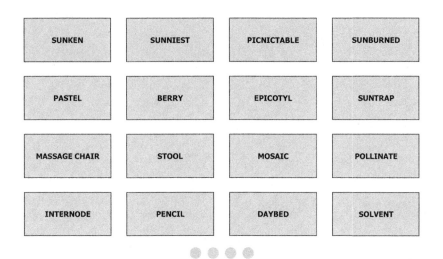

SUNKEN   SUNNIEST   PICNICTABLE   SUNBURNED

PASTEL   BERRY   EPICOTYL   SUNTRAP

MASSAGE CHAIR   STOOL   MOSAIC   POLLINATE

INTERNODE   PENCIL   DAYBED   SOLVENT

Four groups of four words that share something in common :

Group #1 : _____

_____ _____ _____ _____

Group #2 : _____

_____ _____ _____ _____

Group #3 : _____

_____ _____ _____ _____

Group #4 : _____

_____ _____ _____ _____

41

Puzzle # 37

The solution is on page # 214

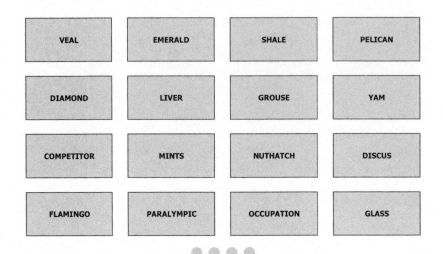

VEAL	EMERALD	SHALE	PELICAN
DIAMOND	LIVER	GROUSE	YAM
COMPETITOR	MINTS	NUTHATCH	DISCUS
FLAMINGO	PARALYMPIC	OCCUPATION	GLASS

Four groups of four words that share something in common :

Group #1 : _____

_____   _____   _____   _____

Group #2 : _____

_____   _____   _____   _____

Group #3 : _____

_____   _____   _____   _____

Group #4 : _____

_____   _____   _____   _____

Puzzle # 38

The solution is on page # 214

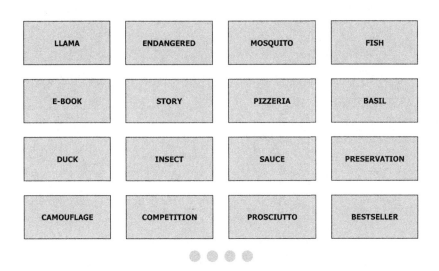

LLAMA	ENDANGERED	MOSQUITO	FISH
E-BOOK	STORY	PIZZERIA	BASIL
DUCK	INSECT	SAUCE	PRESERVATION
CAMOUFLAGE	COMPETITION	PROSCIUTTO	BESTSELLER

Four groups of four words that share something in common :

Group #1 : _____

_____   _____   _____   _____

Group #2 : _____

_____   _____   _____   _____

Group #3 : _____

_____   _____   _____   _____

Group #4 : _____

_____   _____   _____   _____

Puzzle # 39

The solution is on page # 214

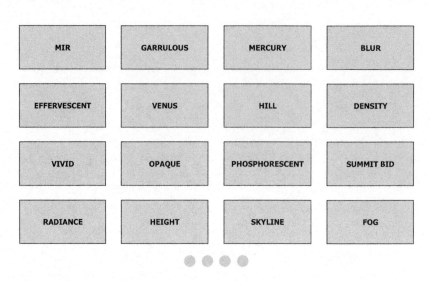

Four groups of four words that share something in common :

Group #1 : _____

_____ _____ _____ _____

Group #2 : _____

_____ _____ _____ _____

Group #3 : _____

_____ _____ _____ _____

Group #4 : _____

_____ _____ _____ _____

Puzzle # 40

The solution is on page # 214

DROP	ONYX	COACHES	BLACKMAIL
SOYBEANS	MELANIN	BLACK BELT	SKI
HOBBY	LASAGNA	IMAGINARY	BESTSELLER
TOFFEE	DYSTOPIA	COOKIE	CHARACTER

Four groups of four words that share something in common :

Group #1 : _____

_____ _____ _____ _____

Group #2 : _____

_____ _____ _____ _____

Group #3 : _____

_____ _____ _____ _____

Group #4 : _____

_____ _____ _____ _____

Puzzle # 41

The solution is on page # 215

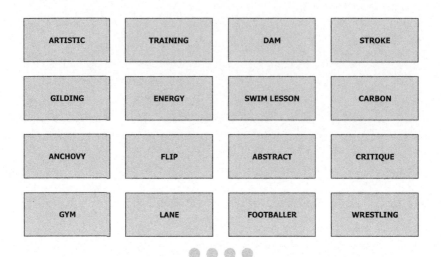

ARTISTIC	TRAINING	DAM	STROKE
GILDING	ENERGY	SWIM LESSON	CARBON
ANCHOVY	FLIP	ABSTRACT	CRITIQUE
GYM	LANE	FOOTBALLER	WRESTLING

Four groups of four words that share something in common :

Group #1 : _____

_____   _____   _____   _____

Group #2 : _____

_____   _____   _____   _____

Group #3 : _____

_____   _____   _____   _____

Group #4 : _____

_____   _____   _____   _____

Puzzle # 42

The solution is on page # 215

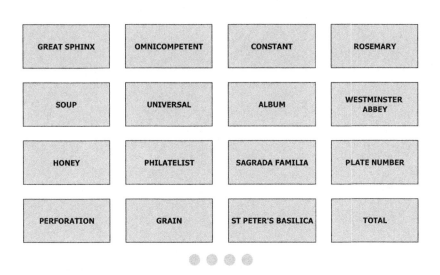

GREAT SPHINX	OMNICOMPETENT	CONSTANT	ROSEMARY
SOUP	UNIVERSAL	ALBUM	WESTMINSTER ABBEY
HONEY	PHILATELIST	SAGRADA FAMILIA	PLATE NUMBER
PERFORATION	GRAIN	ST PETER'S BASILICA	TOTAL

Four groups of four words that share something in common :

Group #1 : _____

_____ _____ _____ _____

Group #2 : _____

_____ _____ _____ _____

Group #3 : _____

_____ _____ _____ _____

Group #4 : _____

_____ _____ _____ _____

Puzzle # 43

The solution is on page # 215

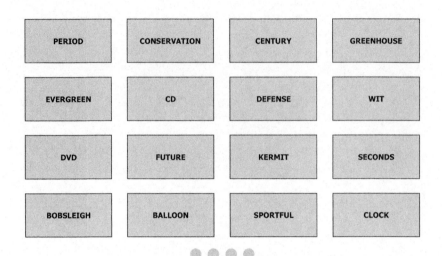

Four groups of four words that share something in common :

Group #1 : _____

_____ _____ _____ _____

Group #2 : _____

_____ _____ _____ _____

Group #3 : _____

_____ _____ _____ _____

Group #4 : _____

_____ _____ _____ _____

Puzzle # 44

The solution is on page # 215

Four groups of four words that share something in common :

Group #1 : _____

_____ _____ _____ _____

Group #2 : _____

_____ _____ _____ _____

Group #3 : _____

_____ _____ _____ _____

Group #4 : _____

_____ _____ _____ _____

Puzzle # 45

The solution is on page # 215

FINE	GLEAMING	ORANGE	HEAVENLY
GAIETY	TERRESTRIAL	ROBUST	WELCOME
BIODIVERSITY	CORNMEAL	JOYOUS	AQUATIC
RAINFOREST	RADIANCE	DOUGH	RIBS

Four groups of four words that share something in common :

Group #1 : _____

_____   _____   _____   _____

Group #2 : _____

_____   _____   _____   _____

Group #3 : _____

_____   _____   _____   _____

Group #4 : _____

_____   _____   _____   _____

Puzzle # 46

The solution is on page # 216

KREMLIN	ROAST	MERINGUE	COLOSSEUM
TECHNOLOGICAL	FLAX	AUGMENTED REALITY	MUSSELS
TECH-SAVVY	GAELIC	TABLE MOUNTAIN	GREEK
AUTOMATION	KURDISH	BERBER	BIG BEN

● ● ● ●

Four groups of four words that share something in common :

Group #1 : _____

_____ _____ _____ _____

Group #2 : _____

_____ _____ _____ _____

Group #3 : _____

_____ _____ _____ _____

Group #4 : _____

_____ _____ _____ _____

Puzzle # 47

The solution is on page # 216

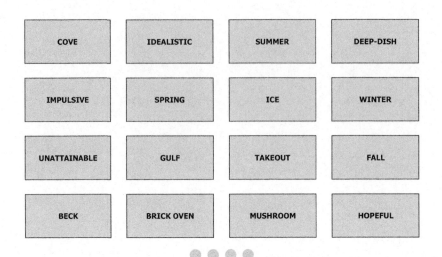

COVE	IDEALISTIC	SUMMER	DEEP-DISH
IMPULSIVE	SPRING	ICE	WINTER
UNATTAINABLE	GULF	TAKEOUT	FALL
BECK	BRICK OVEN	MUSHROOM	HOPEFUL

Four groups of four words that share something in common :

Group #1 : _____

_____   _____   _____   _____

Group #2 : _____

_____   _____   _____   _____

Group #3 : _____

_____   _____   _____   _____

Group #4 : _____

_____   _____   _____   _____

Puzzle # 48

The solution is on page # 216

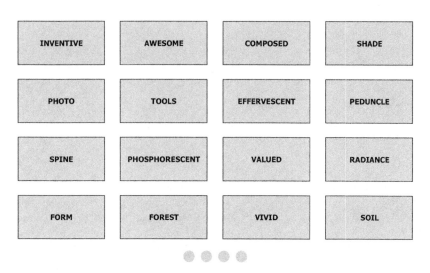

INVENTIVE	AWESOME	COMPOSED	SHADE
PHOTO	TOOLS	EFFERVESCENT	PEDUNCLE
SPINE	PHOSPHORESCENT	VALUED	RADIANCE
FORM	FOREST	VIVID	SOIL

Four groups of four words that share something in common :

Group #1 : _____

_____ _____ _____ _____

Group #2 : _____

_____ _____ _____ _____

Group #3 : _____

_____ _____ _____ _____

Group #4 : _____

_____ _____ _____ _____

Puzzle # 49

The solution is on page # 216

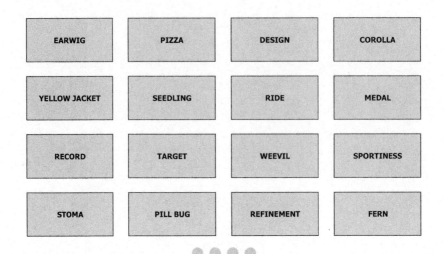

EARWIG	PIZZA	DESIGN	COROLLA
YELLOW JACKET	SEEDLING	RIDE	MEDAL
RECORD	TARGET	WEEVIL	SPORTINESS
STOMA	PILL BUG	REFINEMENT	FERN

Four groups of four words that share something in common :

Group #1 : _____

_____   _____   _____   _____

Group #2 : _____

_____   _____   _____   _____

Group #3 : _____

_____   _____   _____   _____

Group #4 : _____

_____   _____   _____   _____

Puzzle # 50

The solution is on page # 216

ABYSS	BLACKENED	PEAFOWL	ALPHORN
CIRCUMSTANCE	WINDFALL	BLACKSMITH	ALLEGRO
FIDDLE	WINDFALL	GAVIAL	SERENDIPITY
BLACK HOLE	SAW	PIKA	TICK

Four groups of four words that share something in common :

Group #1 : _____

_____ _____ _____ _____

Group #2 : _____

_____ _____ _____ _____

Group #3 : _____

_____ _____ _____ _____

Group #4 : _____

_____ _____ _____ _____

Puzzle # 51

The solution is on page # 217

Four groups of four words that share something in common :

Group #1 : _____

_____   _____   _____   _____

Group #2 : _____

_____   _____   _____   _____

Group #3 : _____

_____   _____   _____   _____

Group #4 : _____

_____   _____   _____   _____

Puzzle # 52

The solution is on page # 217

CORN	ENTHUSIASTIC	ISLANDS	HAPPY
MINIATURE	SALMON	STREAMS	STUBBY
SPUDS	FAT	VOLCANOES	DUNES
THRILLED	SERENE	TALL	CHILI

● ● ● ●

Four groups of four words that share something in common :

Group #1 : _____

_____ _____ _____ _____

Group #2 : _____

_____ _____ _____ _____

Group #3 : _____

_____ _____ _____ _____

Group #4 : _____

_____ _____ _____ _____

Puzzle # 53

The solution is on page # 217

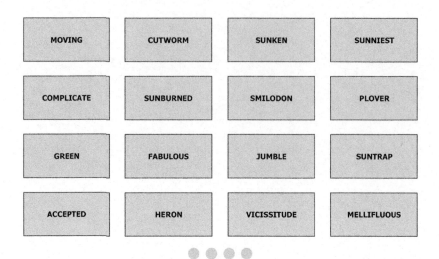

Four groups of four words that share something in common :

Group #1 : _____

_____ _____ _____ _____

Group #2 : _____

_____ _____ _____ _____

Group #3 : _____

_____ _____ _____ _____

Group #4 : _____

_____ _____ _____ _____

Puzzle # 54

The solution is on page # 217

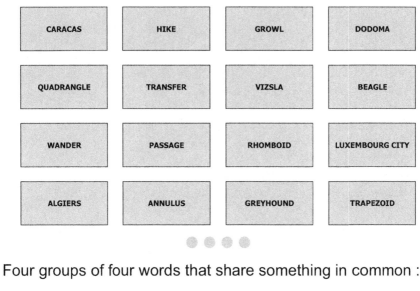

CARACAS	HIKE	GROWL	DODOMA
QUADRANGLE	TRANSFER	VIZSLA	BEAGLE
WANDER	PASSAGE	RHOMBOID	LUXEMBOURG CITY
ALGIERS	ANNULUS	GREYHOUND	TRAPEZOID

Four groups of four words that share something in common :

Group #1 : _____

_____ _____ _____ _____

Group #2 : _____

_____ _____ _____ _____

Group #3 : _____

_____ _____ _____ _____

Group #4 : _____

_____ _____ _____ _____

Puzzle # 55

The solution is on page # 217

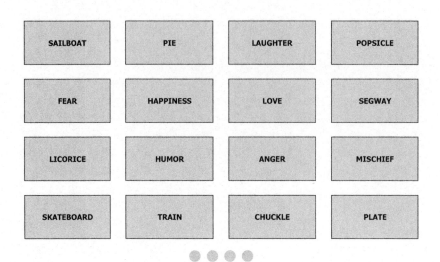

Four groups of four words that share something in common :

Group #1 : _____

_____   _____   _____   _____

Group #2 : _____

_____   _____   _____   _____

Group #3 : _____

_____   _____   _____   _____

Group #4 : _____

_____   _____   _____   _____

Puzzle # 56

The solution is on page # 218

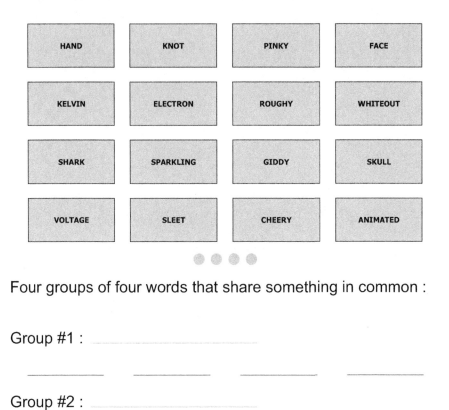

Four groups of four words that share something in common :

Group #1 : _____

_____   _____   _____   _____

Group #2 : _____

_____   _____   _____   _____

Group #3 : _____

_____   _____   _____   _____

Group #4 : _____

_____   _____   _____   _____

Puzzle # 57

The solution is on page # 218

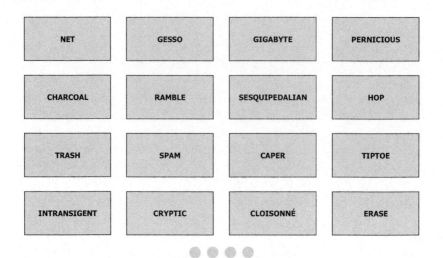

NET	GESSO	GIGABYTE	PERNICIOUS
CHARCOAL	RAMBLE	SESQUIPEDALIAN	HOP
TRASH	SPAM	CAPER	TIPTOE
INTRANSIGENT	CRYPTIC	CLOISONNÉ	ERASE

Four groups of four words that share something in common :

Group #1 : _____

_____   _____   _____   _____

Group #2 : _____

_____   _____   _____   _____

Group #3 : _____

_____   _____   _____   _____

Group #4 : _____

_____   _____   _____   _____

Puzzle # 58

The solution is on page # 218

URSA MAJOR	ILLUMINANT	MARMOSET	FOURTH
SHEEN	COSMIC	POTBELLIEDPIG	LUMINOUS
CIMBALOM	GUPPY	SOLAR	LIZARD
ASTRAL	OCTATONIC	MARCATO	SCINTILLANT

● ● ● ●

Four groups of four words that share something in common :

Group #1 : _____

_____ _____ _____ _____

Group #2 : _____

_____ _____ _____ _____

Group #3 : _____

_____ _____ _____ _____

Group #4 : _____

_____ _____ _____ _____

Puzzle # 59

The solution is on page # 218

HOODIE	ISRAEL	NORWAY	SEOUL
SKOPJE	SINGAPORE	SHAWL	TECHNOLOGY
TURBAN	ESWATINI	PORT-AU-PRINCE	JAPAN
CAP	PRECISION	TIRES	FLY

● ● ● ●

Four groups of four words that share something in common :

Group #1 : _____

_____   _____   _____   _____

Group #2 : _____

_____   _____   _____   _____

Group #3 : _____

_____   _____   _____   _____

Group #4 : _____

_____   _____   _____   _____

Puzzle # 60

The solution is on page # 218

Four groups of four words that share something in common :

Group #1 : _____

_____ _____ _____ _____

Group #2 : _____

_____ _____ _____ _____

Group #3 : _____

_____ _____ _____ _____

Group #4 : _____

_____ _____ _____ _____

Puzzle # 61

The solution is on page # 219

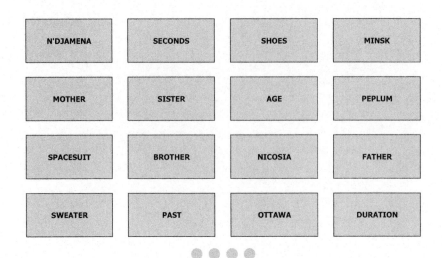

Four groups of four words that share something in common :

Group #1 : _____

_____   _____   _____   _____

Group #2 : _____

_____   _____   _____   _____

Group #3 : _____

_____   _____   _____   _____

Group #4 : _____

_____   _____   _____   _____

Puzzle # 62

The solution is on page # 219

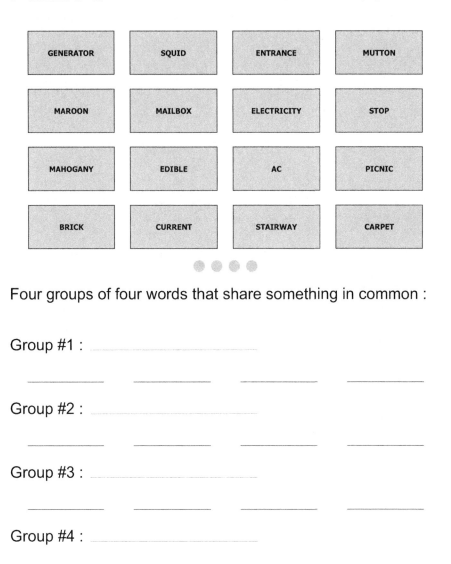

Four groups of four words that share something in common :

Group #1 : _____

_____ _____ _____ _____

Group #2 : _____

_____ _____ _____ _____

Group #3 : _____

_____ _____ _____ _____

Group #4 : _____

_____ _____ _____ _____

Puzzle # 63

The solution is on page # 219

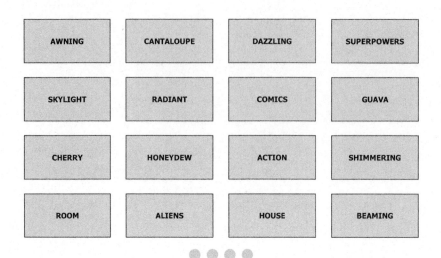

Four groups of four words that share something in common :

Group #1 : _____

_____ _____ _____ _____

Group #2 : _____

_____ _____ _____ _____

Group #3 : _____

_____ _____ _____ _____

Group #4 : _____

_____ _____ _____ _____

Puzzle # 64

The solution is on page # 219

DIATOM	HOOT	MALAWI	BRAZIL
ZEBRA	SKY	ARGENTINA	CHIMPANZEE
STARS	BROWNBEAR	TOUCAN	CANDLELIGHT
RUSSIA	JAGUAR	LEOPARD	ROUNDWORM

● ● ● ●

Four groups of four words that share something in common :

Group #1 : _____

_____ _____ _____ _____

Group #2 : _____

_____ _____ _____ _____

Group #3 : _____

_____ _____ _____ _____

Group #4 : _____

_____ _____ _____ _____

Puzzle # 65

The solution is on page # 219

SKUNK	DREAMER	DREAMINESS	VENEZUELA
TRIANGLE	COD	INDIA	AMBITION
TURKEY	MELODY	FANTASY	FLY
PIPA	PEKINGESE	TREBLE	TUVALU

● ● ● ●

Four groups of four words that share something in common :

Group #1 : _____

_____   _____   _____   _____

Group #2 : _____

_____   _____   _____   _____

Group #3 : _____

_____   _____   _____   _____

Group #4 : _____

_____   _____   _____   _____

Puzzle # 66

The solution is on page # 220

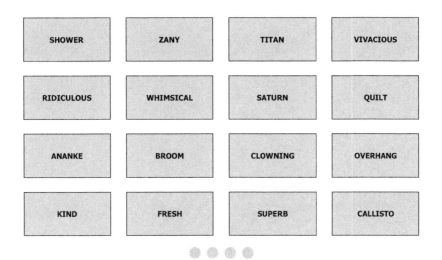

SHOWER	ZANY	TITAN	VIVACIOUS
RIDICULOUS	WHIMSICAL	SATURN	QUILT
ANANKE	BROOM	CLOWNING	OVERHANG
KIND	FRESH	SUPERB	CALLISTO

Four groups of four words that share something in common :

Group #1 : _____

_____ _____ _____ _____

Group #2 : _____

_____ _____ _____ _____

Group #3 : _____

_____ _____ _____ _____

Group #4 : _____

_____ _____ _____ _____

Puzzle # 67

The solution is on page # 220

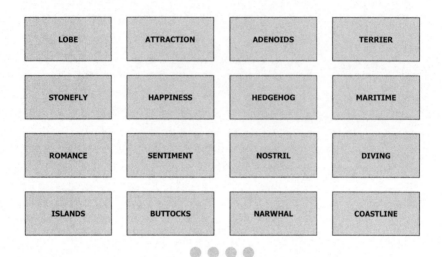

Four groups of four words that share something in common :

Group #1 : _____

_____   _____   _____   _____

Group #2 : _____

_____   _____   _____   _____

Group #3 : _____

_____   _____   _____   _____

Group #4 : _____

_____   _____   _____   _____

Puzzle # 68

The solution is on page # 220

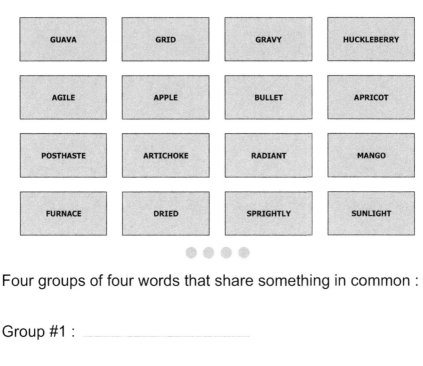

Four groups of four words that share something in common :

Group #1 : _____

_____   _____   _____   _____

Group #2 : _____

_____   _____   _____   _____

Group #3 : _____

_____   _____   _____   _____

Group #4 : _____

_____   _____   _____   _____

Puzzle # 69

The solution is on page # 220

OBSERVATION	BAROMETRIC PRESSURE	RED	EFFULGENT
AERIAL VIEW	RADIANT	SPARKLING	PASTE
FRUIT	LUCID	EFFERVESCENT	REWARDING
ESTEEMED	HONEST	CLIFF	GRILLED

● ● ● ●

Four groups of four words that share something in common :

Group #1 : _____

_____ _____ _____ _____

Group #2 : _____

_____ _____ _____ _____

Group #3 : _____

_____ _____ _____ _____

Group #4 : _____

_____ _____ _____ _____

74

Puzzle # 70

The solution is on page # 220

NIAMEY	KIGALI	JOUSTING	YOGA
FORM	GUATEMALA CITY	DOMAIN	ISLAMABAD
SCREEN	CARS	TOOLS	SCRIPT
CROSS	PHOTO	COMMAND	SHADE

● ● ● ●

Four groups of four words that share something in common :

Group #1 : _____

_____ _____ _____ _____

Group #2 : _____

_____ _____ _____ _____

Group #3 : _____

_____ _____ _____ _____

Group #4 : _____

_____ _____ _____ _____

Puzzle # 71

The solution is on page # 221

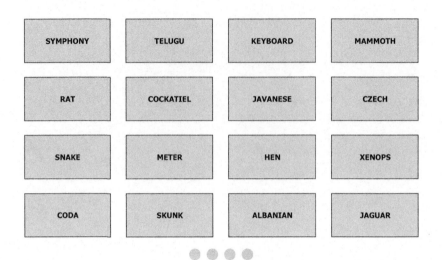

Four groups of four words that share something in common :

Group #1 : _____

_____ _____ _____ _____

Group #2 : _____

_____ _____ _____ _____

Group #3 : _____

_____ _____ _____ _____

Group #4 : _____

_____ _____ _____ _____

Puzzle # 72

The solution is on page # 221

INTERLOCK	ITINERARY	PORTICO	RAPPORT
BOWLING	CROSSING	WAGGERY	TOUR
TOILET	POPULAR	POOL	INTERDEPENDENCE
GAMEDAY	LINK	WALKWAY	ODYSSEY

● ● ● ●

Four groups of four words that share something in common :

Group #1 : _____

_____   _____   _____   _____

Group #2 : _____

_____   _____   _____   _____

Group #3 : _____

_____   _____   _____   _____

Group #4 : _____

_____   _____   _____   _____

Puzzle # 73

The solution is on page # 221

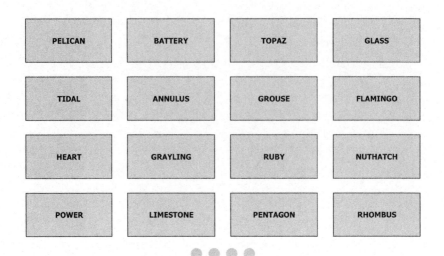

Four groups of four words that share something in common :

Group #1 : _____

_____ _____ _____ _____

Group #2 : _____

_____ _____ _____ _____

Group #3 : _____

_____ _____ _____ _____

Group #4 : _____

_____ _____ _____ _____

Puzzle # 74

The solution is on page # 221

NAVEL	FILTER	NECK	PROFUSION
POLARIZER	PLENITUDE	PYONGYANG	DJIBOUTI
RULE OF THIRDS	KUALA LUMPUR	SANTO DOMINGO	EYEBROW
COPIOUS	ABOUNDING	FILLING	APERTURE

● ● ● ●

Four groups of four words that share something in common :

Group #1 : _____

_____ _____ _____ _____

Group #2 : _____

_____ _____ _____ _____

Group #3 : _____

_____ _____ _____ _____

Group #4 : _____

_____ _____ _____ _____

Puzzle # 75

The solution is on page # 221

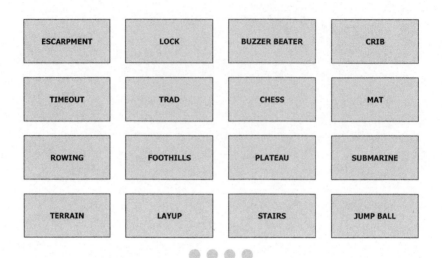

Four groups of four words that share something in common :

Group #1 : _____

_____ _____ _____ _____

Group #2 : _____

_____ _____ _____ _____

Group #3 : _____

_____ _____ _____ _____

Group #4 : _____

_____ _____ _____ _____

Puzzle # 76

The solution is on page # 222

YOGURT	CONFUSION	BILLIARDS	ENDIVE
ANTICIPATION	ANXIETY	SHELF	ATHLETICS
FEAR	COOKBOOK	RECREATION	HOBBIES
SHOT	SCORE	PUBLISHER	BRAN

● ● ● ●

Four groups of four words that share something in common :

Group #1 : _____

_____   _____   _____   _____

Group #2 : _____

_____   _____   _____   _____

Group #3 : _____

_____   _____   _____   _____

Group #4 : _____

_____   _____   _____   _____

Puzzle # 77

The solution is on page # 222

PROGRESS	MOTORCYCLE	INTERNET	LAKE
BERBER	NETWORKING	LAPTOP	HANGGLIDER
WATERCOURSE	AIRPLANE	KURDISH	TRAIN
GAELIC	WATERCOURSE	GREEK	WATERFALL

● ● ● ●

Four groups of four words that share something in common :

Group #1 : _____

_____ _____ _____ _____

Group #2 : _____

_____ _____ _____ _____

Group #3 : _____

_____ _____ _____ _____

Group #4 : _____

_____ _____ _____ _____

Puzzle # 78

The solution is on page # 222

PAGE-TURNER	COAL	EPHEMERAL	INCIDENTAL
FACE	IMAGINATION	CLIMAX	SETTING
STURGEON	SHORT-LIVED	HASTY	PINKY
SKULL	HAND	RENEWABLE	LOACH

Four groups of four words that share something in common :

Group #1 : _____

_____ _____ _____ _____

Group #2 : _____

_____ _____ _____ _____

Group #3 : _____

_____ _____ _____ _____

Group #4 : _____

_____ _____ _____ _____

Puzzle # 79

The solution is on page # 222

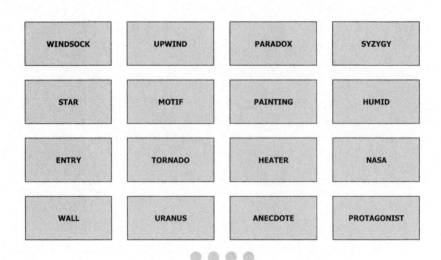

Four groups of four words that share something in common :

Group #1 : _____

_____   _____   _____   _____

Group #2 : _____

_____   _____   _____   _____

Group #3 : _____

_____   _____   _____   _____

Group #4 : _____

_____   _____   _____   _____

Puzzle # 80

The solution is on page # 222

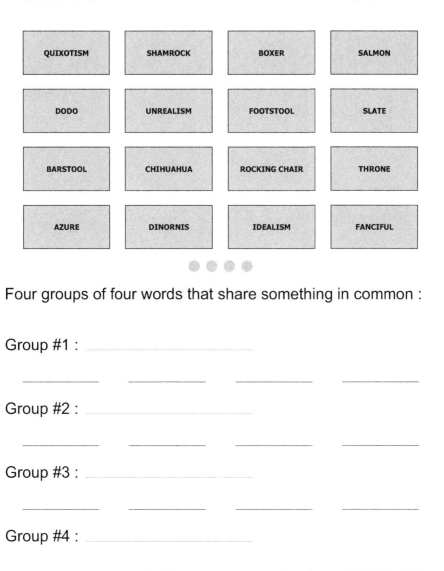

Four groups of four words that share something in common :

Group #1 : _____

_____ _____ _____ _____

Group #2 : _____

_____ _____ _____ _____

Group #3 : _____

_____ _____ _____ _____

Group #4 : _____

_____ _____ _____ _____

Puzzle # 81

The solution is on page # 223

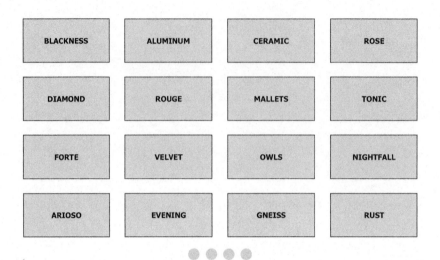

Four groups of four words that share something in common :

Group #1 : _____

_____ _____ _____ _____

Group #2 : _____

_____ _____ _____ _____

Group #3 : _____

_____ _____ _____ _____

Group #4 : _____

_____ _____ _____ _____

Puzzle # 82

The solution is on page # 223

ANDANTINO	NIGHTCAP	RING	BOW
INSOMNIA	PIECHART	HARMONICS	MOON
CAMERA	PASSWORD	RINGTONE	VUVUZELA
SLEEP	PANCAKE	AIRPLANE MODE	NIGHT SKY

● ● ● ●

Four groups of four words that share something in common :

Group #1 : _____

_____ _____ _____ _____

Group #2 : _____

_____ _____ _____ _____

Group #3 : _____

_____ _____ _____ _____

Group #4 : _____

_____ _____ _____ _____

87

Puzzle # 83

The solution is on page # 223

GIRAFFE	RUN	ELAND	COLOSSAL
BASS	PACE	MERCEDES	CRUISE
PETROL	ULTIMATE	NABARLEK	SLENDER
LANKY	STROLL	GIANT	SPRINT

Four groups of four words that share something in common :

Group #1 : _____

_____   _____   _____   _____

Group #2 : _____

_____   _____   _____   _____

Group #3 : _____

_____   _____   _____   _____

Group #4 : _____

_____   _____   _____   _____

Puzzle # 84

The solution is on page # 223

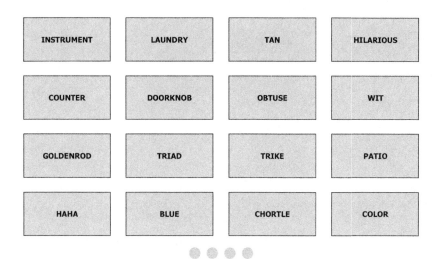

INSTRUMENT	LAUNDRY	TAN	HILARIOUS
COUNTER	DOORKNOB	OBTUSE	WIT
GOLDENROD	TRIAD	TRIKE	PATIO
HAHA	BLUE	CHORTLE	COLOR

Four groups of four words that share something in common :

Group #1 : _____

_____ _____ _____ _____

Group #2 : _____

_____ _____ _____ _____

Group #3 : _____

_____ _____ _____ _____

Group #4 : _____

_____ _____ _____ _____

Puzzle # 85

The solution is on page # 223

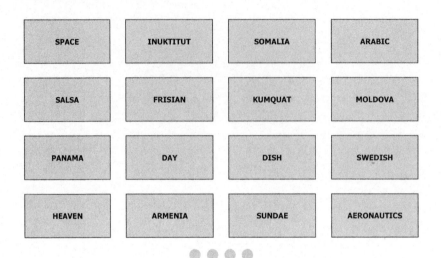

SPACE	INUKTITUT	SOMALIA	ARABIC
SALSA	FRISIAN	KUMQUAT	MOLDOVA
PANAMA	DAY	DISH	SWEDISH
HEAVEN	ARMENIA	SUNDAE	AERONAUTICS

Four groups of four words that share something in common :

Group #1 : _____

_____ _____ _____ _____

Group #2 : _____

_____ _____ _____ _____

Group #3 : _____

_____ _____ _____ _____

Group #4 : _____

_____ _____ _____ _____

Puzzle # 86

The solution is on page # 224

MADURESE	BRICK	RUBY	GERMAN
CAR	GOLFCART	SPANISH	UZBEK
ROLLERSKATES	SAPPHIRE	INSTANT	ZEPPELIN
CLASSICAL	RESTORED	BEAUTIFUL	JASPER

● ● ● ●

Four groups of four words that share something in common :

Group #1 : _____

_____ _____ _____ _____

Group #2 : _____

_____ _____ _____ _____

Group #3 : _____

_____ _____ _____ _____

Group #4 : _____

_____ _____ _____ _____

Puzzle # 87

The solution is on page # 224

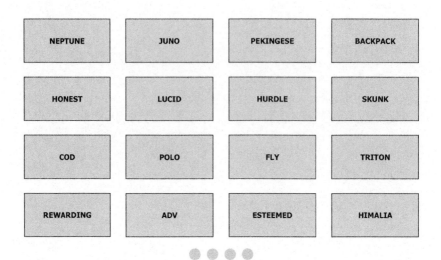

NEPTUNE	JUNO	PEKINGESE	BACKPACK
HONEST	LUCID	HURDLE	SKUNK
COD	POLO	FLY	TRITON
REWARDING	ADV	ESTEEMED	HIMALIA

Four groups of four words that share something in common :

Group #1 : _____

_____ _____ _____ _____

Group #2 : _____

_____ _____ _____ _____

Group #3 : _____

_____ _____ _____ _____

Group #4 : _____

_____ _____ _____ _____

Puzzle # 88

The solution is on page # 224

EDITOR	CHASING WINDMILLS	HERRING	BOOKMARK
TRIFECTA	IMAGINARY	IDEALIZED	MUSICAL
MANDRILL	BUSHBABY	GAME	ROMANTIC
MOUSE	TRIGONOMETRY	PENROSE	NARRATOR

● ● ● ●

Four groups of four words that share something in common :

Group #1 : _____

_____ _____ _____ _____

Group #2 : _____

_____ _____ _____ _____

Group #3 : _____

_____ _____ _____ _____

Group #4 : _____

_____ _____ _____ _____

Puzzle # 89

The solution is on page # 224

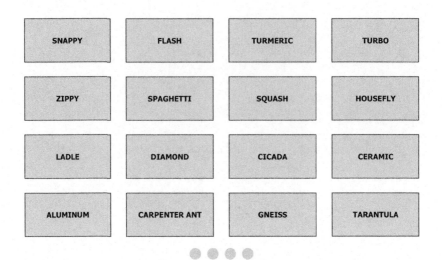

Four groups of four words that share something in common :

Group #1 : _____

_____ _____ _____ _____

Group #2 : _____

_____ _____ _____ _____

Group #3 : _____

_____ _____ _____ _____

Group #4 : _____

_____ _____ _____ _____

Puzzle # 90

The solution is on page # 224

BRILLIANT	BEET	LUMINOUS	APERTURE
VACUUM	SOLAR	TEMPORANEOUS	GREENBEANS
GLISTER	PARALLAX	GARLIC	SCALLION
HASTY	IMPERMANENT	EFFULGENT	INTERMITTENT

● ● ● ●

Four groups of four words that share something in common :

Group #1 : _____

_____   _____   _____   _____

Group #2 : _____

_____   _____   _____   _____

Group #3 : _____

_____   _____   _____   _____

Group #4 : _____

_____   _____   _____   _____

Puzzle # 91

The solution is on page # 225

DESIRE	TURKISH	DREAMED	EMOJI
BASQUE	WATERCOURSE	TOUCHSCREEN	INTERNET
LAKE	HMONG	DANISH	DREAMER
WATERCOURSE	IMAGINATION	WATERFALL	BLUETOOTH

Four groups of four words that share something in common :

Group #1 : _____

_____   _____   _____   _____

Group #2 : _____

_____   _____   _____   _____

Group #3 : _____

_____   _____   _____   _____

Group #4 : _____

_____   _____   _____   _____

Puzzle # 92

The solution is on page # 225

DISSEMBLE	CRUST	AMBIGUOUS	JUICE
CAPRESE	SHRIMP	HAZE	SUNBATH
SAUTÉED	CHOW	SOY	SUNSETTING
SOLANUM LYCOPERSICUM	SUNLIT	SUNUP	MYSTIFY

● ● ● ●

Four groups of four words that share something in common :

Group #1 : _____

_____   _____   _____   _____

Group #2 : _____

_____   _____   _____   _____

Group #3 : _____

_____   _____   _____   _____

Group #4 : _____

_____   _____   _____   _____

Puzzle # 93

The solution is on page # 225

Four groups of four words that share something in common :

Group #1 : _____

_____ _____ _____ _____

Group #2 : _____

_____ _____ _____ _____

Group #3 : _____

_____ _____ _____ _____

Group #4 : _____

_____ _____ _____ _____

Puzzle # 94

The solution is on page # 225

ROCKING CHAIR	ENCYCLOPEDIA	FOOTSTOOL	THESIS
HIGH	PICCOLO	MANUSCRIPT	THRONE
CELLO	ALMANAC	NEXRAD	RAINSTICK
CYCLONE	BARSTOOL	BIOGRAPHY	MOLTO

● ● ● ●

Four groups of four words that share something in common :

Group #1 : _____

_____ _____ _____ _____

Group #2 : _____

_____ _____ _____ _____

Group #3 : _____

_____ _____ _____ _____

Group #4 : _____

_____ _____ _____ _____

Puzzle # 95

The solution is on page # 225

TINY	THEATRICAL LIGHTING	PROPS	ACTOR
HUMOR	THIN	SMILE	JAGUAR
APPLAUSE	HEN	SHORT	MERRYMENT
XENOPS	HOHO	CURVY	MAMMOTH

● ● ● ●

Four groups of four words that share something in common :

Group #1 : _____

_____ _____ _____ _____

Group #2 : _____

_____ _____ _____ _____

Group #3 : _____

_____ _____ _____ _____

Group #4 : _____

_____ _____ _____ _____

Puzzle # 96

The solution is on page # 226

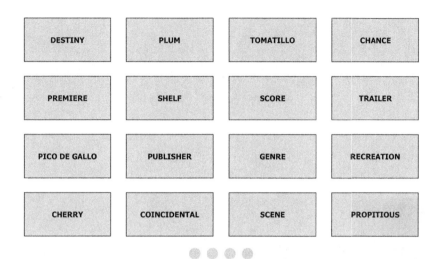

Four groups of four words that share something in common :

Group #1 : _____

_____ _____ _____ _____

Group #2 : _____

_____ _____ _____ _____

Group #3 : _____

_____ _____ _____ _____

Group #4 : _____

_____ _____ _____ _____

Puzzle # 97

The solution is on page # 226

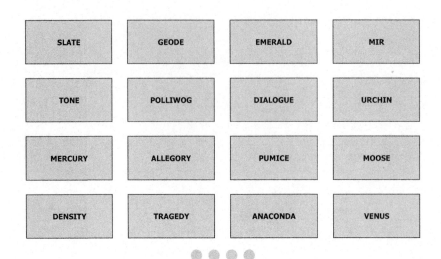

SLATE	GEODE	EMERALD	MIR
TONE	POLLIWOG	DIALOGUE	URCHIN
MERCURY	ALLEGORY	PUMICE	MOOSE
DENSITY	TRAGEDY	ANACONDA	VENUS

Four groups of four words that share something in common :

Group #1 : _____

_____ _____ _____ _____

Group #2 : _____

_____ _____ _____ _____

Group #3 : _____

_____ _____ _____ _____

Group #4 : _____

_____ _____ _____ _____

Puzzle # 98

The solution is on page # 226

MASTERFUL	MALTESE	FIG	SHOOTER
WOW	CASSEROLE	TRUTHFUL	DAIKON
SCHUSS	IBIBIO	AFRIKAANS	POSITION
WORKING	ACTIVE	ENGLISH	SALAD

Four groups of four words that share something in common :

Group #1 : _____

_____ _____ _____ _____

Group #2 : _____

_____ _____ _____ _____

Group #3 : _____

_____ _____ _____ _____

Group #4 : _____

_____ _____ _____ _____

103

Puzzle # 99

The solution is on page # 226

ITINERARY	CROSSING	ORATORICAL	ECUADOR
ODYSSEY	GRANDILOQUENT	LAOS	WHITE PIZZA
PROLIX	FAMILY-SIZED	FETA	TOUR
CIRCUMLOCUTION	NIGERIA	OLIVE OIL	CUBA

● ● ● ●

Four groups of four words that share something in common :

Group #1 : _____

_____   _____   _____   _____

Group #2 : _____

_____   _____   _____   _____

Group #3 : _____

_____   _____   _____   _____

Group #4 : _____

_____   _____   _____   _____

Puzzle # 100

The solution is on page # 226

FRIDAY	SATURDAY	LOVESEAT	SPORT
CELLPHONE	AUTUMN	BREAKFAST	TOUCH ID
DO NOT DISTURB	COMPETITION	TUFFET	BEANBAG CHAIR
VOICE ASSISTANT	FAN	RECLINER	MANUSCRIPT

● ● ● ●

Four groups of four words that share something in common :

Group #1 : _____

_____   _____   _____   _____

Group #2 : _____

_____   _____   _____   _____

Group #3 : _____

_____   _____   _____   _____

Group #4 : _____

_____   _____   _____   _____

Puzzle # 101

The solution is on page # 227

DREAMY	BRIEF	BRACELET	VALLEYS
SHORT-TERM	TREE LINE	CREST	LOOKOUT
SLIP	RAPID	ECCENTRIC	BOW
CHIVALROUS	FROCK	EXTRAVAGANT	BRIEF

● ● ● ●

Four groups of four words that share something in common :

Group #1 : _____

_____ _____ _____ _____

Group #2 : _____

_____ _____ _____ _____

Group #3 : _____

_____ _____ _____ _____

Group #4 : _____

_____ _____ _____ _____

106

Puzzle # 102

The solution is on page # 227

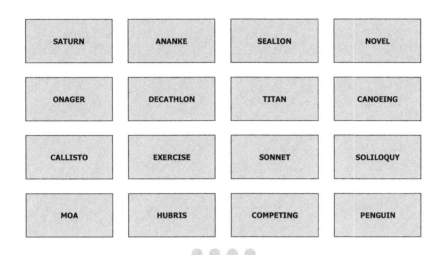

Four groups of four words that share something in common :

Group #1 : _____

_____   _____   _____   _____

Group #2 : _____

_____   _____   _____   _____

Group #3 : _____

_____   _____   _____   _____

Group #4 : _____

_____   _____   _____   _____

Puzzle # 103

The solution is on page # 227

Four groups of four words that share something in common :

Group #1 : _____

_____ _____ _____ _____

Group #2 : _____

_____ _____ _____ _____

Group #3 : _____

_____ _____ _____ _____

Group #4 : _____

_____ _____ _____ _____

Puzzle # 104

The solution is on page # 227

SPORE	ELEVATION GAIN	CANOPY	KERCHIEF
HOUSECOAT	GEOGRAPHIC COORDINATES	PINEAPPLE	PADDLE
MARINARA	CULOTTES	HIGH	KILT
WHORLED	KUDZU	MOSS	GARLIC

Four groups of four words that share something in common :

Group #1 : _____

_____ _____ _____ _____

Group #2 : _____

_____ _____ _____ _____

Group #3 : _____

_____ _____ _____ _____

Group #4 : _____

_____ _____ _____ _____

Puzzle # 105

The solution is on page # 227

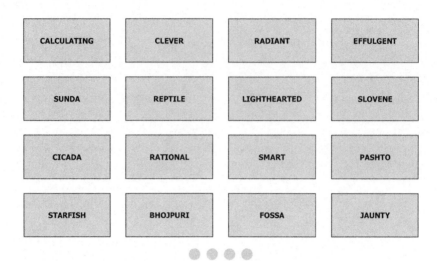

CALCULATING	CLEVER	RADIANT	EFFULGENT
SUNDA	REPTILE	LIGHTHEARTED	SLOVENE
CICADA	RATIONAL	SMART	PASHTO
STARFISH	BHOJPURI	FOSSA	JAUNTY

Four groups of four words that share something in common :

Group #1 : _____

_____ _____ _____ _____

Group #2 : _____

_____ _____ _____ _____

Group #3 : _____

_____ _____ _____ _____

Group #4 : _____

_____ _____ _____ _____

Puzzle # 106

The solution is on page # 228

ELECTRON	KIT	SHARK	NOMENCLATURE
JUDO	SPORT	CARDIGAN	ONESIES
MIDDLE NAME	MENTION	ZORIS	PRACTICE
RECOGNITION	DISPORT	ROUGHY	VOLTAGE

● ● ● ●

Four groups of four words that share something in common :

Group #1 : _____

_____ _____ _____ _____

Group #2 : _____

_____ _____ _____ _____

Group #3 : _____

_____ _____ _____ _____

Group #4 : _____

_____ _____ _____ _____

Puzzle # 107

The solution is on page # 228

FANTASY	BOOK	JUBA	ADDIS ABABA
PARABLE	MYTH	BOUT	WHODUNIT
NORMAL	MAGAZINE	AUTOBIOGRAPHY	WORKOUT
MALABO	MORONI	WORLD	ALMANAC

● ● ● ●

Four groups of four words that share something in common :

Group #1 : _____

_____ _____ _____ _____

Group #2 : _____

_____ _____ _____ _____

Group #3 : _____

_____ _____ _____ _____

Group #4 : _____

_____ _____ _____ _____

Puzzle # 108

The solution is on page # 228

MERRY	IRREPRESSIBLE	DESIGN	SUIT
BREECHES	TOGA	HONEY	EBULLIENT
ROSEMARY	GALOSHES	SOUP	GRAIN
SPORTINESS	RIDE	REFINEMENT	JUBILANT

● ● ● ●

Four groups of four words that share something in common :

Group #1 : _____

_____   _____   _____   _____

Group #2 : _____

_____   _____   _____   _____

Group #3 : _____

_____   _____   _____   _____

Group #4 : _____

_____   _____   _____   _____

113

Puzzle # 109

The solution is on page # 228

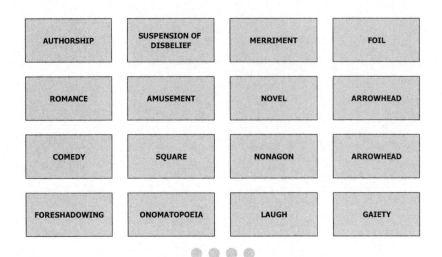

Four groups of four words that share something in common :

Group #1 : _____

_____ _____ _____ _____

Group #2 : _____

_____ _____ _____ _____

Group #3 : _____

_____ _____ _____ _____

Group #4 : _____

_____ _____ _____ _____

Puzzle # 110

The solution is on page # 228

AMHARIC	AUTHORSHIP	ROMANCE	DREAMLIKE
YIDDISH	DAYDREAM	NOVEL	DREAMER
DREAMED	SOMALI	NOOK	SUSPENSION OF DISBELIEF
PLUMBING	TETUM	BATHTUB	STOVE

● ● ● ●

Four groups of four words that share something in common :

Group #1 : _____

_____ _____ _____ _____

Group #2 : _____

_____ _____ _____ _____

Group #3 : _____

_____ _____ _____ _____

Group #4 : _____

_____ _____ _____ _____

Puzzle # 111

The solution is on page # 229

EUPHORIC	ZESTFUL	STRATUS	CHESS
CELESTIAL	METEOROLOGY	TROPOSPHERE	EXHILARATED
CHARMED	ROWING	ISO	BRACKETING
SUBMARINE	MEGAPIXELS	TRAD	SHUTTER SPEED

Four groups of four words that share something in common :

Group #1 : _____

_____ _____ _____ _____

Group #2 : _____

_____ _____ _____ _____

Group #3 : _____

_____ _____ _____ _____

Group #4 : _____

_____ _____ _____ _____

Puzzle # 112

The solution is on page # 229

FLEA	RIVER	LINEN	ACRYLIC
FAIR	SAND FLY	NORMAL	DRIZZLE
STILL LIFE	FOLIAGE	WIND	COLD
JUNE BUG	CENTIPEDE	SEASHELLS	MEDIUM

● ● ● ●

Four groups of four words that share something in common :

Group #1 : _____

_____   _____   _____   _____

Group #2 : _____

_____   _____   _____   _____

Group #3 : _____

_____   _____   _____   _____

Group #4 : _____

_____   _____   _____   _____

Puzzle # 113

The solution is on page # 229

JADE	LOVE	PIZZAIOLO	ANACONDA
IRON	CRISPY	CURIOSITY	SAPPHIRE
TAKEOUT	CORUNDUM	URCHIN	POLLIWOG
OREGANO	IRRITATION	RESENTMENT	MOOSE

● ● ● ●

Four groups of four words that share something in common :

Group #1 : _____

_____ _____ _____ _____

Group #2 : _____

_____ _____ _____ _____

Group #3 : _____

_____ _____ _____ _____

Group #4 : _____

_____ _____ _____ _____

Puzzle # 114

The solution is on page # 229

PETRIFIEDWOOD	CORUNDUM	ALLIGATOR	KISMET
COINCIDENTAL	PREDESTINATION	EON	BASALT
EPHEMERON	COATI	TEMPORANEOUS	SHORT-LIVED
KUDU	EORAPTOR	TOPAZ	HAPPENSTANCE

Four groups of four words that share something in common :

Group #1 : _____

_____ _____ _____ _____

Group #2 : _____

_____ _____ _____ _____

Group #3 : _____

_____ _____ _____ _____

Group #4 : _____

_____ _____ _____ _____

Puzzle # 115

The solution is on page # 229

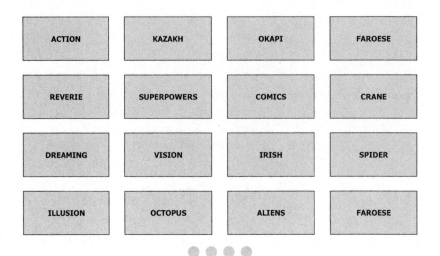

ACTION	KAZAKH	OKAPI	FAROESE
REVERIE	SUPERPOWERS	COMICS	CRANE
DREAMING	VISION	IRISH	SPIDER
ILLUSION	OCTOPUS	ALIENS	FAROESE

Four groups of four words that share something in common :

Group #1 : _____

_____ _____ _____ _____

Group #2 : _____

_____ _____ _____ _____

Group #3 : _____

_____ _____ _____ _____

Group #4 : _____

_____ _____ _____ _____

Puzzle # 116

The solution is on page # 230

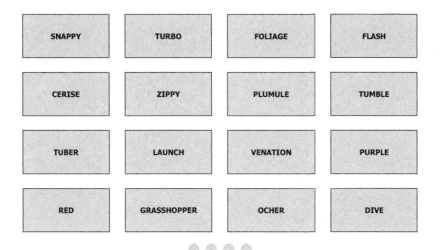

Four groups of four words that share something in common :

Group #1 : _____

_____ _____ _____ _____

Group #2 : _____

_____ _____ _____ _____

Group #3 : _____

_____ _____ _____ _____

Group #4 : _____

_____ _____ _____ _____

Puzzle # 117

The solution is on page # 230

DILI	SALAD	BLISSFUL	POLLIWOG
ROSEAU	GLAD	HEIRLOOM	RAPTUROUS
URCHIN	BEEFSTEAK	WINDHOEK	CHEERY
MOOSE	GREEN	BUDAPEST	ANACONDA

Four groups of four words that share something in common :

Group #1 : _____

_____ _____ _____ _____

Group #2 : _____

_____ _____ _____ _____

Group #3 : _____

_____ _____ _____ _____

Group #4 : _____

_____ _____ _____ _____

Puzzle # 118

The solution is on page # 230

CREEK	LABYRINTHINE	OCEAN	EFFULGENT
ULTRA	BRILLIANT	ABERRATION	LUMINOUS
OPAQUE	NOTEWORTHY	QUIXOTIC	ARM
AIRPLANE	GLISTER	OXBOW	PERFORM

Four groups of four words that share something in common :

Group #1 : _____

_____   _____   _____   _____

Group #2 : _____

_____   _____   _____   _____

Group #3 : _____

_____   _____   _____   _____

Group #4 : _____

_____   _____   _____   _____

123

Puzzle # 119

The solution is on page # 230

BUNS	SOFTWARE	OMNIVORE	ARTIFICIAL INTELLIGENCE
CREATIVE	NUTRIENT	OBFUSCATE	POPULAR
SMARTPHONE	CONSTANT	JULIENNE	MYSTIFY
RECALCITRANT	PERPLEXITY	NURTURING	CUTTING-EDGE

● ● ● ●

Four groups of four words that share something in common :

Group #1 : _____

_____ _____ _____ _____

Group #2 : _____

_____ _____ _____ _____

Group #3 : _____

_____ _____ _____ _____

Group #4 : _____

_____ _____ _____ _____

Puzzle # 120

The solution is on page # 230

STARS   BALALAIKA   NIGHT   TABLE OF CONTENTS

PLOT   HURDYGURDY   STADIUM   HORNET

CARNIVORA   FICTION   POMPANO   SAXOPHONE

GOLDFINCH   KALIMBA   SOLAR SYSTEM   ALTITUDE

Four groups of four words that share something in common :

Group #1 : _____

_____ _____ _____ _____

Group #2 : _____

_____ _____ _____ _____

Group #3 : _____

_____ _____ _____ _____

Group #4 : _____

_____ _____ _____ _____

Puzzle # 121

The solution is on page # 231

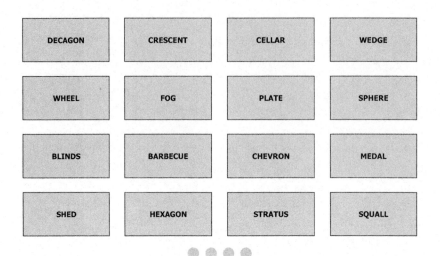

Four groups of four words that share something in common :

Group #1 : _____

_____ _____ _____ _____

Group #2 : _____

_____ _____ _____ _____

Group #3 : _____

_____ _____ _____ _____

Group #4 : _____

_____ _____ _____ _____

Puzzle # 122

The solution is on page # 231

INTERLOCK	INTERDEPENDENCE	SCREWBALL	KHASIPAPEDA
GAG	LINK	FINGER LIME	OWLS
EXAGGERATION	EVENING	KABOSU	KEY LIME
RAPPORT	BLACKNESS	ECCENTRIC	NIGHTFALL

● ● ● ●

Four groups of four words that share something in common :

Group #1 : _____

_____ _____ _____ _____

Group #2 : _____

_____ _____ _____ _____

Group #3 : _____

_____ _____ _____ _____

Group #4 : _____

_____ _____ _____ _____

Puzzle # 123

The solution is on page # 231

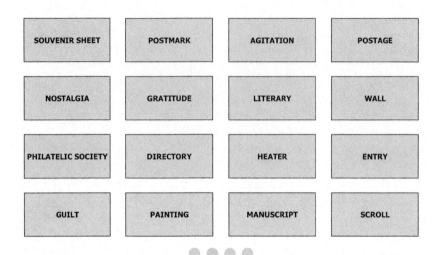

SOUVENIR SHEET	POSTMARK	AGITATION	POSTAGE
NOSTALGIA	GRATITUDE	LITERARY	WALL
PHILATELIC SOCIETY	DIRECTORY	HEATER	ENTRY
GUILT	PAINTING	MANUSCRIPT	SCROLL

Four groups of four words that share something in common :

Group #1 : _____

_____   _____   _____   _____

Group #2 : _____

_____   _____   _____   _____

Group #3 : _____

_____   _____   _____   _____

Group #4 : _____

_____   _____   _____   _____

Puzzle # 124

The solution is on page # 231

NIGHTCAP	BOOT	YAK	CRUNCH
SHALLOTS	ROBE	TIGER	PARKA
OWL	SLEEP	NIGHT SKY	HORSE
OLEO	DINER	TROUSERS	INSOMNIA

● ● ● ●

Four groups of four words that share something in common :

Group #1 : _____

_____   _____   _____   _____

Group #2 : _____

_____   _____   _____   _____

Group #3 : _____

_____   _____   _____   _____

Group #4 : _____

_____   _____   _____   _____

129

Puzzle # 125

The solution is on page # 231

GREEN	AUBURN	CLOGS	SAFETY
TRANSPORT	GOLD	MONTEVIDEO	BUCKLE
DHAKA	RIGA	EARRINGS	FEELING
MBABANE	OVERSHIRT	EXCELLENCE	RUSSET

● ● ● ●

Four groups of four words that share something in common :

Group #1 : _____

_____   _____   _____   _____

Group #2 : _____

_____   _____   _____   _____

Group #3 : _____

_____   _____   _____   _____

Group #4 : _____

_____   _____   _____   _____

Puzzle # 126

The solution is on page # 232

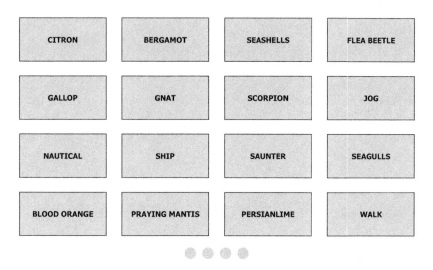

CITRON	BERGAMOT	SEASHELLS	FLEA BEETLE
GALLOP	GNAT	SCORPION	JOG
NAUTICAL	SHIP	SAUNTER	SEAGULLS
BLOOD ORANGE	PRAYING MANTIS	PERSIANLIME	WALK

Four groups of four words that share something in common :

Group #1 : _____

_____ _____ _____ _____

Group #2 : _____

_____ _____ _____ _____

Group #3 : _____

_____ _____ _____ _____

Group #4 : _____

_____ _____ _____ _____

Puzzle # 127

The solution is on page # 232

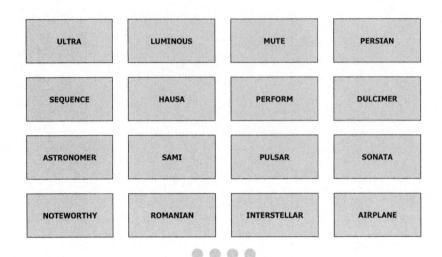

Four groups of four words that share something in common :

Group #1 : _____

_____ _____ _____ _____

Group #2 : _____

_____ _____ _____ _____

Group #3 : _____

_____ _____ _____ _____

Group #4 : _____

_____ _____ _____ _____

Puzzle # 128

The solution is on page # 232

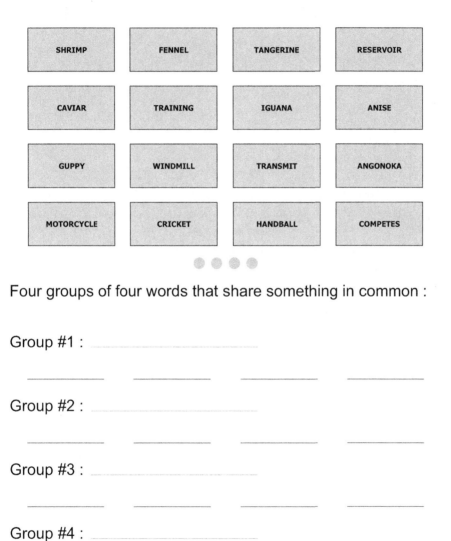

Four groups of four words that share something in common :

Group #1 : _____

_____ _____ _____ _____

Group #2 : _____

_____ _____ _____ _____

Group #3 : _____

_____ _____ _____ _____

Group #4 : _____

_____ _____ _____ _____

Puzzle # 129

The solution is on page # 232

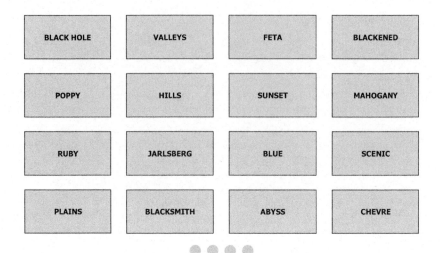

Four groups of four words that share something in common :

Group #1 : _____

_____   _____   _____   _____

Group #2 : _____

_____   _____   _____   _____

Group #3 : _____

_____   _____   _____   _____

Group #4 : _____

_____   _____   _____   _____

Puzzle # 130

The solution is on page # 232

SHIRT	NEXUS	LIBYA	TRANSIT
SPORTSTER	INTERCONNECTION	INTEGRATION	YEMEN
BRIDGE	COSTUME	LAPEL	BOOST
ANGOLA	EXPENSIVE	UNDERWEAR	MALDIVES

Four groups of four words that share something in common :

Group #1 : _____

_____ _____ _____ _____

Group #2 : _____

_____ _____ _____ _____

Group #3 : _____

_____ _____ _____ _____

Group #4 : _____

_____ _____ _____ _____

Puzzle # 131

The solution is on page # 233

Four groups of four words that share something in common :

Group #1 : _____

_____ _____ _____ _____

Group #2 : _____

_____ _____ _____ _____

Group #3 : _____

_____ _____ _____ _____

Group #4 : _____

_____ _____ _____ _____

Puzzle # 132

The solution is on page # 233

BREAST	CELL	SWEETPOTATO	LEG
TARSAL	HAPPINESS	APPLE	SHAME
RUST	BRICK	RADISH	SPINACH
SADNESS	JICAMA	FOXY	AFFECTION

● ● ● ●

Four groups of four words that share something in common :

Group #1 : _____

_____   _____   _____   _____

Group #2 : _____

_____   _____   _____   _____

Group #3 : _____

_____   _____   _____   _____

Group #4 : _____

_____   _____   _____   _____

Puzzle # 133

The solution is on page # 233

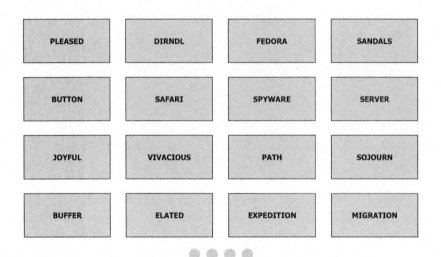

PLEASED	DIRNDL	FEDORA	SANDALS
BUTTON	SAFARI	SPYWARE	SERVER
JOYFUL	VIVACIOUS	PATH	SOJOURN
BUFFER	ELATED	EXPEDITION	MIGRATION

Four groups of four words that share something in common :

Group #1 : _____

_____ _____ _____ _____

Group #2 : _____

_____ _____ _____ _____

Group #3 : _____

_____ _____ _____ _____

Group #4 : _____

_____ _____ _____ _____

Puzzle # 134

The solution is on page # 233

CATERPILLAR	MIGRATION	RESTORATION	KATYDID
MADURESE	GERMAN	ELAND	NABARLEK
SPANISH	BASS	UZBEK	GIRAFFE
DRAGONFLY	MIDGE	EXTINCTION	ECOSYSTEM

Four groups of four words that share something in common :

Group #1 : _____

_____ _____ _____ _____

Group #2 : _____

_____ _____ _____ _____

Group #3 : _____

_____ _____ _____ _____

Group #4 : _____

_____ _____ _____ _____

Puzzle # 135

The solution is on page # 233

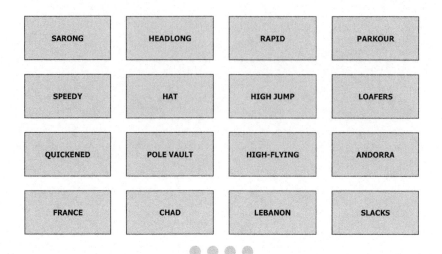

SARONG	HEADLONG	RAPID	PARKOUR
SPEEDY	HAT	HIGH JUMP	LOAFERS
QUICKENED	POLE VAULT	HIGH-FLYING	ANDORRA
FRANCE	CHAD	LEBANON	SLACKS

Four groups of four words that share something in common :

Group #1 : _____

_____ _____ _____ _____

Group #2 : _____

_____ _____ _____ _____

Group #3 : _____

_____ _____ _____ _____

Group #4 : _____

_____ _____ _____ _____

Puzzle # 136

The solution is on page # 234

BEAN	TOTAL	KIMONO	COVER
FEZ	MISLEAD	SHAMROCK	SNEAKERS
ALL-AROUND	NECTAR	SCREEN	PERENNIAL
PERVADING	NETTED	TRUCULENT	CLOAK

● ● ● ●

Four groups of four words that share something in common :

Group #1 : _____

_____ _____ _____ _____

Group #2 : _____

_____ _____ _____ _____

Group #3 : _____

_____ _____ _____ _____

Group #4 : _____

_____ _____ _____ _____

Puzzle # 137

The solution is on page # 234

QUINOA	BLACKENED CHICKEN	CHARCOAL	GREENBEANS
SHADOW	PLATTER	GYRO	SPICES
GARLIC	RINGS	HERB	CORK
STEALTH	SEPAL	BEET	SCALLION

● ● ● ●

Four groups of four words that share something in common :

Group #1 : _____

_____ _____ _____ _____

Group #2 : _____

_____ _____ _____ _____

Group #3 : _____

_____ _____ _____ _____

Group #4 : _____

_____ _____ _____ _____

Puzzle # 138

The solution is on page # 234

Four groups of four words that share something in common :

Group #1 : _____

_____ _____ _____ _____

Group #2 : _____

_____ _____ _____ _____

Group #3 : _____

_____ _____ _____ _____

Group #4 : _____

_____ _____ _____ _____

Puzzle # 139

The solution is on page # 234

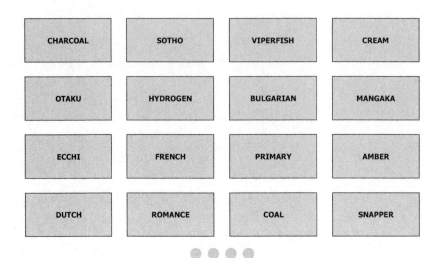

Four groups of four words that share something in common :

Group #1 : _____

_____ _____ _____ _____

Group #2 : _____

_____ _____ _____ _____

Group #3 : _____

_____ _____ _____ _____

Group #4 : _____

_____ _____ _____ _____

Puzzle # 140

The solution is on page # 234

Four groups of four words that share something in common :

Group #1 : _____

_____ _____ _____ _____

Group #2 : _____

_____ _____ _____ _____

Group #3 : _____

_____ _____ _____ _____

Group #4 : _____

_____ _____ _____ _____

Puzzle # 141

The solution is on page # 235

Four groups of four words that share something in common :

Group #1 : _____

_____ _____ _____ _____

Group #2 : _____

_____ _____ _____ _____

Group #3 : _____

_____ _____ _____ _____

Group #4 : _____

_____ _____ _____ _____

Puzzle # 142

The solution is on page # 235

LIMITED	SEPTEMBER	TICK	CHRISTMAS
SPORTER	MAY	TAMIL	GAVIAL
JANUARY	PIKA	FILIPINO	OFFSIDE
MAORI	SUBBUTEO	NORWEGIAN	PEAFOWL

● ● ● ●

Four groups of four words that share something in common :

Group #1 : _____

_____   _____   _____   _____

Group #2 : _____

_____   _____   _____   _____

Group #3 : _____

_____   _____   _____   _____

Group #4 : _____

_____   _____   _____   _____

Puzzle # 143

The solution is on page # 235

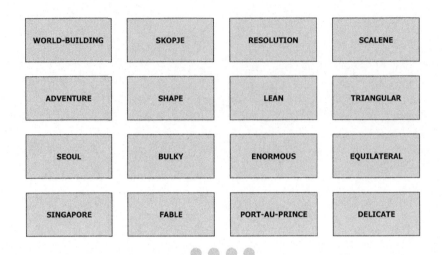

Four groups of four words that share something in common :

Group #1 : _____

_____   _____   _____   _____

Group #2 : _____

_____   _____   _____   _____

Group #3 : _____

_____   _____   _____   _____

Group #4 : _____

_____   _____   _____   _____

Puzzle # 144

The solution is on page # 235

PIANO	EFFULGENT	FIRETRUCK	SPARKLING
GLOCKENSPIEL	RADIANT	REDTULIP	OXBOW
OBOE	CHERRY	EFFERVESCENT	TRUMPET
CREEK	STRAWBERRY	ARM	OCEAN

Four groups of four words that share something in common :

Group #1 : _____

_____ _____ _____ _____

Group #2 : _____

_____ _____ _____ _____

Group #3 : _____

_____ _____ _____ _____

Group #4 : _____

_____ _____ _____ _____

149

Puzzle # 145

The solution is on page # 235

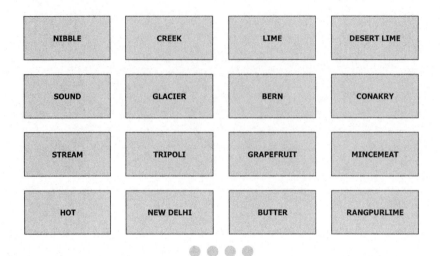

NIBBLE | CREEK | LIME | DESERT LIME

SOUND | GLACIER | BERN | CONAKRY

STREAM | TRIPOLI | GRAPEFRUIT | MINCEMEAT

HOT | NEW DELHI | BUTTER | RANGPURLIME

Four groups of four words that share something in common :

Group #1 : _____

_____ _____ _____ _____

Group #2 : _____

_____ _____ _____ _____

Group #3 : _____

_____ _____ _____ _____

Group #4 : _____

_____ _____ _____ _____

Puzzle # 146

The solution is on page # 236

UKULELE	PREMIUM	PASTIME	TABLA
QUIRK	TRAIN	SOCIAL	HANGGLIDER
TRILL	CORNET	AIRPLANE	HAPPENSTANCE
NONGAME	MOTORCYCLE	FORTUITY	FORTUNATE

Four groups of four words that share something in common :

Group #1 : _____

_____   _____   _____   _____

Group #2 : _____

_____   _____   _____   _____

Group #3 : _____

_____   _____   _____   _____

Group #4 : _____

_____   _____   _____   _____

151

Puzzle # 147

The solution is on page # 236

PIGMENT	WATERCOLOR	RAPIDS	COBBLER
RAPIDS	GESSO	ECRU	GARLIC
LIME	VARNISH	APRICOT	RIVER
VIRIDIAN	ARM	PASTA	PAN

Four groups of four words that share something in common :

Group #1 : _____

_____ _____ _____ _____

Group #2 : _____

_____ _____ _____ _____

Group #3 : _____

_____ _____ _____ _____

Group #4 : _____

_____ _____ _____ _____

Puzzle # 148

The solution is on page # 236

MALAYSIA	CANOPY	ELEVATION GAIN	WEASEL
BOTSWANA	SCORE	GEOGRAPHIC COORDINATES	TORTOISE
USA	TURTLE	CAMEROON	RECREATION
SHELF	PUBLISHER	EDENTA	HIGH

● ● ● ●

Four groups of four words that share something in common :

Group #1 : _____

_____ _____ _____ _____

Group #2 : _____

_____ _____ _____ _____

Group #3 : _____

_____ _____ _____ _____

Group #4 : _____

_____ _____ _____ _____

Puzzle # 149

The solution is on page # 236

STAND-UP	SHOULDER	MACAW	MODEM
BETAFISH	AMUSING	LIGHTHEARTED	PRANK
ANUS	TISSUE	OFFLINE	USERNAME
TEETH	BEARDEDDRAGON	CONFIGURE	GUINEAPIG

● ● ● ●

Four groups of four words that share something in common :

Group #1 : _____

_____ _____ _____ _____

Group #2 : _____

_____ _____ _____ _____

Group #3 : _____

_____ _____ _____ _____

Group #4 : _____

_____ _____ _____ _____

Puzzle # 150

The solution is on page # 236

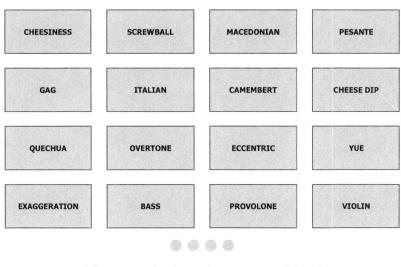

Four groups of four words that share something in common :

Group #1 : _____

_____ _____ _____ _____

Group #2 : _____

_____ _____ _____ _____

Group #3 : _____

_____ _____ _____ _____

Group #4 : _____

_____ _____ _____ _____

Puzzle # 151

The solution is on page # 237

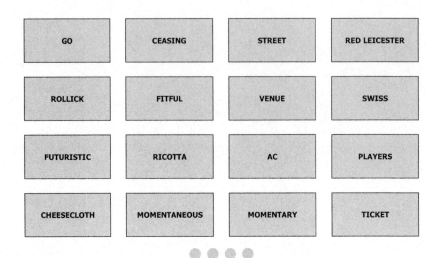

GO	CEASING	STREET	RED LEICESTER
ROLLICK	FITFUL	VENUE	SWISS
FUTURISTIC	RICOTTA	AC	PLAYERS
CHEESECLOTH	MOMENTANEOUS	MOMENTARY	TICKET

Four groups of four words that share something in common :

Group #1 : _____

_____   _____   _____   _____

Group #2 : _____

_____   _____   _____   _____

Group #3 : _____

_____   _____   _____   _____

Group #4 : _____

_____   _____   _____   _____

Puzzle # 152

The solution is on page # 237

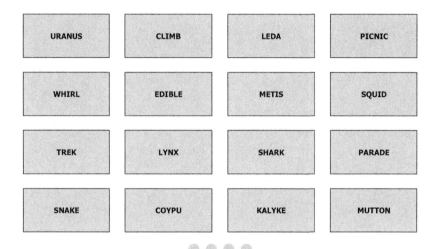

URANUS	CLIMB	LEDA	PICNIC
WHIRL	EDIBLE	METIS	SQUID
TREK	LYNX	SHARK	PARADE
SNAKE	COYPU	KALYKE	MUTTON

Four groups of four words that share something in common :

Group #1 : _____

_____   _____   _____   _____

Group #2 : _____

_____   _____   _____   _____

Group #3 : _____

_____   _____   _____   _____

Group #4 : _____

_____   _____   _____   _____

157

Puzzle # 153

The solution is on page # 237

BUCHAREST	CHANNEL	CHANNEL	THIRST
WETLAND	MARMALADE	SEMPRE	NATURAL
BELL	NUKU'ALOFA	ANDORRA LA VELLA	OUAGADOUGOU
FERMATA	BARBECUE	BLAND	FOOD

Four groups of four words that share something in common :

Group #1 : _____

_____ _____ _____ _____

Group #2 : _____

_____ _____ _____ _____

Group #3 : _____

_____ _____ _____ _____

Group #4 : _____

_____ _____ _____ _____

Puzzle # 154

The solution is on page # 237

FLAMBOYANT	CUPBOARD	HTML	COMMUNICATION
GLARE	SNACK	FOLDER	ATTACHMENT
HOOKUP	MIRROR	LINK	GLITTERING
COOK	AFFILIATION	TURNIP	DAZZLING

● ● ● ●

Four groups of four words that share something in common :

Group #1 : _____

_____   _____   _____   _____

Group #2 : _____

_____   _____   _____   _____

Group #3 : _____

_____   _____   _____   _____

Group #4 : _____

_____   _____   _____   _____

Puzzle # 155

The solution is on page # 237

FICKLE	SCAN	CLOAK	TREK
CAMOUFLAGE	DRAG	ROAMING	PORTAL
EPHEMERAL	LAPSE	EPHEMERAL	TRAVEL
XENOPHOBIA	DISCOVERY	EQUANIMITY	CD

Four groups of four words that share something in common :

Group #1 : _____

_____ _____ _____ _____

Group #2 : _____

_____ _____ _____ _____

Group #3 : _____

_____ _____ _____ _____

Group #4 : _____

_____ _____ _____ _____

Puzzle # 156

The solution is on page # 238

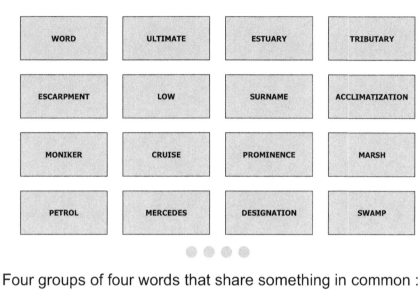

WORD	ULTIMATE	ESTUARY	TRIBUTARY
ESCARPMENT	LOW	SURNAME	ACCLIMATIZATION
MONIKER	CRUISE	PROMINENCE	MARSH
PETROL	MERCEDES	DESIGNATION	SWAMP

Four groups of four words that share something in common :

Group #1 : _____

_____ _____ _____ _____

Group #2 : _____

_____ _____ _____ _____

Group #3 : _____

_____ _____ _____ _____

Group #4 : _____

_____ _____ _____ _____

Puzzle # 157

The solution is on page # 238

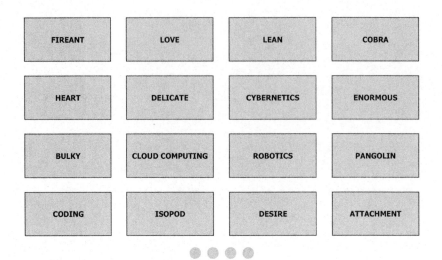

Four groups of four words that share something in common :

Group #1 : _____

_____ _____ _____ _____

Group #2 : _____

_____ _____ _____ _____

Group #3 : _____

_____ _____ _____ _____

Group #4 : _____

_____ _____ _____ _____

Puzzle # 158

The solution is on page # 238

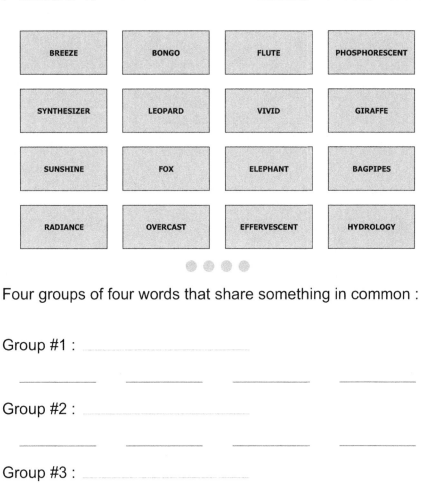

Four groups of four words that share something in common :

Group #1 : _____

_____ _____ _____ _____

Group #2 : _____

_____ _____ _____ _____

Group #3 : _____

_____ _____ _____ _____

Group #4 : _____

_____ _____ _____ _____

Puzzle # 159

The solution is on page # 238

Four groups of four words that share something in common :

Group #1 : _____

_____   _____   _____   _____

Group #2 : _____

_____   _____   _____   _____

Group #3 : _____

_____   _____   _____   _____

Group #4 : _____

_____   _____   _____   _____

Puzzle # 160

The solution is on page # 238

CHINA	VIOLIN	PESANTE	EUROPA
DREAM	OVERTONE	CHARON	SYRIA
BASS	SINOPE	SINGAPORE	DREAMLAND
UTOPIA	DREAMCATCHER	AUSTRALIA	RHEA

● ● ● ●

Four groups of four words that share something in common :

Group #1 : _____

_____ _____ _____ _____

Group #2 : _____

_____ _____ _____ _____

Group #3 : _____

_____ _____ _____ _____

Group #4 : _____

_____ _____ _____ _____

Puzzle # 161

The solution is on page # 239

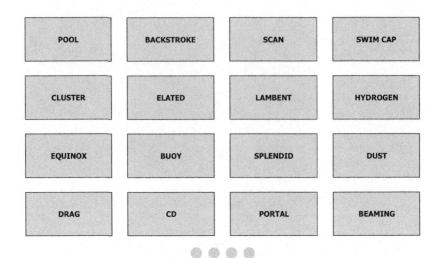

POOL	BACKSTROKE	SCAN	SWIM CAP
CLUSTER	ELATED	LAMBENT	HYDROGEN
EQUINOX	BUOY	SPLENDID	DUST
DRAG	CD	PORTAL	BEAMING

Four groups of four words that share something in common :

Group #1 : _____

_____   _____   _____   _____

Group #2 : _____

_____   _____   _____   _____

Group #3 : _____

_____   _____   _____   _____

Group #4 : _____

_____   _____   _____   _____

Puzzle # 162

The solution is on page # 239

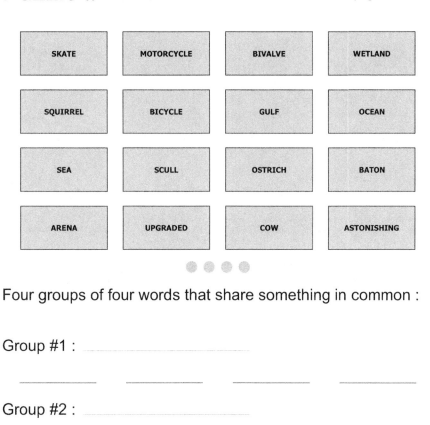

SKATE	MOTORCYCLE	BIVALVE	WETLAND
SQUIRREL	BICYCLE	GULF	OCEAN
SEA	SCULL	OSTRICH	BATON
ARENA	UPGRADED	COW	ASTONISHING

Four groups of four words that share something in common :

Group #1 : _____

_____ _____ _____ _____

Group #2 : _____

_____ _____ _____ _____

Group #3 : _____

_____ _____ _____ _____

Group #4 : _____

_____ _____ _____ _____

167

Puzzle # 163

The solution is on page # 239

BATTER | MANAGUA | EXPERIENCE | CHAMELEON

GAMESOME | DISCOVERY | DROMEDARY | EXPEDITION

BRUSSELS | KINSHASA | MEERKAT | PICKLEBALL

CHICKADEE | QUEST | PACK | NGERULMUD

Four groups of four words that share something in common :

Group #1 : _____

_____ _____ _____ _____

Group #2 : _____

_____ _____ _____ _____

Group #3 : _____

_____ _____ _____ _____

Group #4 : _____

_____ _____ _____ _____

Puzzle # 164

The solution is on page # 239

ARM	CAPILLARY	BLAND	TOWER BRIDGE
DONKEY	FEMUR	ANIMAL	BARBECUE
FOOD	WOODCHUCK	PARTHENON	ALHAMBRA
EAGLE	MARMALADE	FOREHEAD	ANGKOR WAT

Four groups of four words that share something in common :

Group #1 : _____

_____ _____ _____ _____

Group #2 : _____

_____ _____ _____ _____

Group #3 : _____

_____ _____ _____ _____

Group #4 : _____

_____ _____ _____ _____

Puzzle # 165

The solution is on page # 239

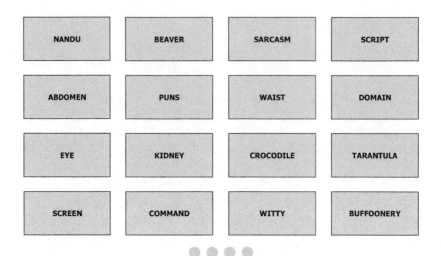

NANDU | BEAVER | SARCASM | SCRIPT

ABDOMEN | PUNS | WAIST | DOMAIN

EYE | KIDNEY | CROCODILE | TARANTULA

SCREEN | COMMAND | WITTY | BUFFOONERY

Four groups of four words that share something in common :

Group #1 : _____

_____ _____ _____ _____

Group #2 : _____

_____ _____ _____ _____

Group #3 : _____

_____ _____ _____ _____

Group #4 : _____

_____ _____ _____ _____

Puzzle # 166

The solution is on page # 240

JUDO	SPORT	YAREN DISTRICT	PANAMA CITY
MARSH	SIZZLE	ANCHOVIES	CHEESE
GLACIERS	ECOSYSTEM	NASSAU	SLICE
DISPORT	PRACTICE	BANGUI	WILDLIFE

● ● ● ●

Four groups of four words that share something in common :

Group #1 : _____

_____   _____   _____   _____

Group #2 : _____

_____   _____   _____   _____

Group #3 : _____

_____   _____   _____   _____

Group #4 : _____

_____   _____   _____   _____

171

Puzzle # 167

The solution is on page # 240

COURTSHIP	SETTING	PANTYHOSE	INFATUATION
SOCK	FEELING	SYMBOLISM	STREAM OF CONSCIOUSNESS
INVERSION	RAINBOW	LOW	SNOWSTORM
BONNET	JUMPSUIT	NARRATOR	CONNECTION

● ● ● ●

Four groups of four words that share something in common :

Group #1 : _____

_____ _____ _____ _____

Group #2 : _____

_____ _____ _____ _____

Group #3 : _____

_____ _____ _____ _____

Group #4 : _____

_____ _____ _____ _____

172

Puzzle # 168

The solution is on page # 240

CUPCAKE	TORSO	INDIA	TURKEY
TUX	WAISTCOAT	KOHLRABI	TUVALU
DRESS	TONSILS	JUMPER	LUNCHMEAT
WRIST	SHERBET	TOE	VENEZUELA

Four groups of four words that share something in common :

Group #1 : _____

_____ _____ _____ _____

Group #2 : _____

_____ _____ _____ _____

Group #3 : _____

_____ _____ _____ _____

Group #4 : _____

_____ _____ _____ _____

Puzzle # 169

The solution is on page # 240

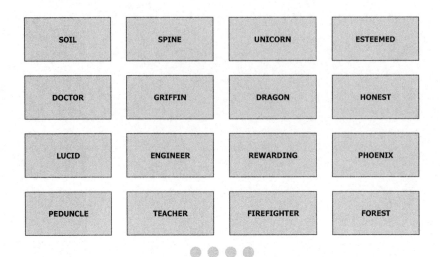

SOIL	SPINE	UNICORN	ESTEEMED
DOCTOR	GRIFFIN	DRAGON	HONEST
LUCID	ENGINEER	REWARDING	PHOENIX
PEDUNCLE	TEACHER	FIREFIGHTER	FOREST

Four groups of four words that share something in common :

Group #1 : _____

_____   _____   _____   _____

Group #2 : _____

_____   _____   _____   _____

Group #3 : _____

_____   _____   _____   _____

Group #4 : _____

_____   _____   _____   _____

Puzzle # 170

The solution is on page # 240

SUNBATHED	JUPITER	CONSTELLATION	KITCHEN
STARLIGHT	REVOLVE	FENCE	METEOR
SUNRAY	SINK	SUNKEN	STARRY-EYED
TRELLIS	DAYLIGHT	METEOROID	ORION

Four groups of four words that share something in common :

Group #1 : _____

_____   _____   _____   _____

Group #2 : _____

_____   _____   _____   _____

Group #3 : _____

_____   _____   _____   _____

Group #4 : _____

_____   _____   _____   _____

Puzzle # 171

The solution is on page # 241

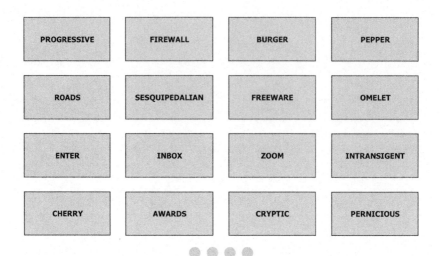

PROGRESSIVE	FIREWALL	BURGER	PEPPER
ROADS	SESQUIPEDALIAN	FREEWARE	OMELET
ENTER	INBOX	ZOOM	INTRANSIGENT
CHERRY	AWARDS	CRYPTIC	PERNICIOUS

Four groups of four words that share something in common :

Group #1 : _____

_____   _____   _____   _____

Group #2 : _____

_____   _____   _____   _____

Group #3 : _____

_____   _____   _____   _____

Group #4 : _____

_____   _____   _____   _____

Puzzle # 172

The solution is on page # 241

EFFICIENT	ERMINE	DIESEL	ERGONOMIC
FUNCTIONAL	NEIGHING	ACCELERATION	EARTHWORM
BRAYING	CRAPPIE	NUMBAT	ROARING
BLEATING	TESLA	MONOTREME	PETROLEUM

● ● ● ●

Four groups of four words that share something in common :

Group #1 : _____

_____ _____ _____ _____

Group #2 : _____

_____ _____ _____ _____

Group #3 : _____

_____ _____ _____ _____

Group #4 : _____

_____ _____ _____ _____

Puzzle # 173

The solution is on page # 241

WORK	BUTTERNUTSQUASH	WOODBALL	BRAWNY
HUSKY	SLIM	MUSCULAR	POSTSEASON
CORN	BELLPEPPER	ARUGULA	JOGGER
GALAGOS	BAT	NARROW	DALMATIAN

● ● ● ●

Four groups of four words that share something in common :

Group #1 : _____

_____ _____ _____ _____

Group #2 : _____

_____ _____ _____ _____

Group #3 : _____

_____ _____ _____ _____

Group #4 : _____

_____ _____ _____ _____

Puzzle # 174

The solution is on page # 241

ENDURO	ECRU	EPHEMERAL	DOORKNOB
FLEETING	BASE	VIRIDIAN	PASSING
LIME	LAUNDRY	APRICOT	OLYMPICS
RAPID	COUNTER	NETBALL	PATIO

Four groups of four words that share something in common :

Group #1 : _____

_____ _____ _____ _____

Group #2 : _____

_____ _____ _____ _____

Group #3 : _____

_____ _____ _____ _____

Group #4 : _____

_____ _____ _____ _____

179

Puzzle # 175

The solution is on page # 241

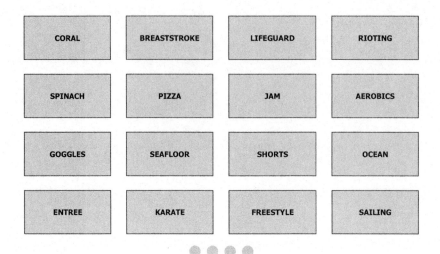

CORAL	BREASTSTROKE	LIFEGUARD	RIOTING
SPINACH	PIZZA	JAM	AEROBICS
GOGGLES	SEAFLOOR	SHORTS	OCEAN
ENTREE	KARATE	FREESTYLE	SAILING

Four groups of four words that share something in common :

Group #1 : _____

_____   _____   _____   _____

Group #2 : _____

_____   _____   _____   _____

Group #3 : _____

_____   _____   _____   _____

Group #4 : _____

_____   _____   _____   _____

Puzzle # 176

The solution is on page # 242

MIRROR	HOME	LAMP	WHIPPET
TOE	CALVES	UNGULATES	FEET
COTTAGE	BEAM	PARMESAN	THIGHS
ROBIN	PIRANHA	EMMENTAL	CHEESIEST

● ● ● ●

Four groups of four words that share something in common :

Group #1 : _____

_____ _____ _____ _____

Group #2 : _____

_____ _____ _____ _____

Group #3 : _____

_____ _____ _____ _____

Group #4 : _____

_____ _____ _____ _____

Puzzle # 177

The solution is on page # 242

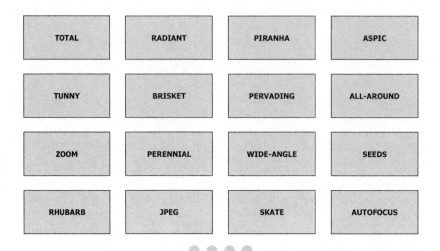

TOTAL	RADIANT	PIRANHA	ASPIC
TUNNY	BRISKET	PERVADING	ALL-AROUND
ZOOM	PERENNIAL	WIDE-ANGLE	SEEDS
RHUBARB	JPEG	SKATE	AUTOFOCUS

Four groups of four words that share something in common :

Group #1 : _____

_____ _____ _____ _____

Group #2 : _____

_____ _____ _____ _____

Group #3 : _____

_____ _____ _____ _____

Group #4 : _____

_____ _____ _____ _____

Puzzle # 178

The solution is on page # 242

MOLDOVA	PANAMA	WEBSITE	NORMAL
MEDIUM	SOMALIA	ARTIST	COLD
ARMENIA	FAIR	UTILITY	QUEUE
CREATE	JAVA	DESIGN	DRIZZLE

● ● ● ●

Four groups of four words that share something in common :

Group #1 : _____

_____   _____   _____   _____

Group #2 : _____

_____   _____   _____   _____

Group #3 : _____

_____   _____   _____   _____

Group #4 : _____

_____   _____   _____   _____

Puzzle # 179

The solution is on page # 242

SHADOWS	MOONLIGHT	TWILIGHT	CHANCE
RECTANGLE	BIOMASS	TRIANGLE	CIRCLE
SQUARE	MEANTIME	WATT	NOCTURNE
SYNCHRONICITY	CARP	REFLECT	UNEXPECTED

● ● ● ●

Four groups of four words that share something in common :

Group #1 : _____

_____ _____ _____ _____

Group #2 : _____

_____ _____ _____ _____

Group #3 : _____

_____ _____ _____ _____

Group #4 : _____

_____ _____ _____ _____

Puzzle # 180

The solution is on page # 242

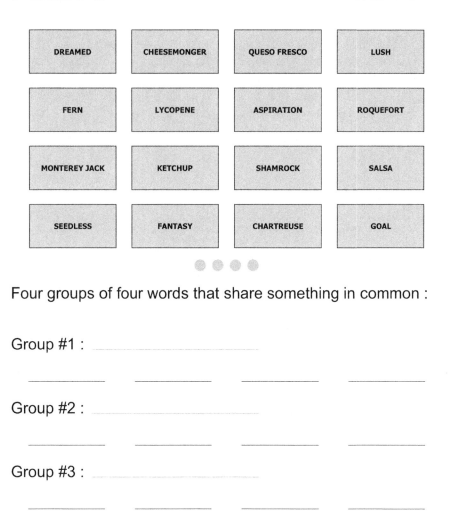

Four groups of four words that share something in common :

Group #1 : _____

_____   _____   _____   _____

Group #2 : _____

_____   _____   _____   _____

Group #3 : _____

_____   _____   _____   _____

Group #4 : _____

_____   _____   _____   _____

Puzzle # 181

The solution is on page # 243

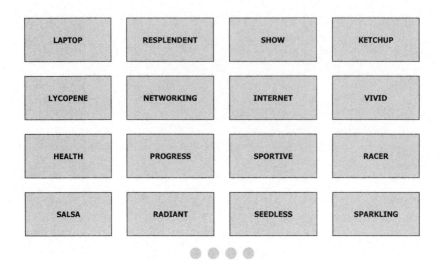

Four groups of four words that share something in common :

Group #1 : _____

_____ _____ _____ _____

Group #2 : _____

_____ _____ _____ _____

Group #3 : _____

_____ _____ _____ _____

Group #4 : _____

_____ _____ _____ _____

Puzzle # 182

The solution is on page # 243

BRICK	GESSO	POWER	SWORDFISH
HELICON	PIGMENT	FLAT	WATERCOLOR
REED	ZEBRAFISH	ETHANOL	HEMATITE
QUARTZ	CONCRETE	BANJO	VARNISH

● ● ● ●

Four groups of four words that share something in common :

Group #1 : _____

_____ _____ _____ _____

Group #2 : _____

_____ _____ _____ _____

Group #3 : _____

_____ _____ _____ _____

Group #4 : _____

_____ _____ _____ _____

Puzzle # 183

The solution is on page # 243

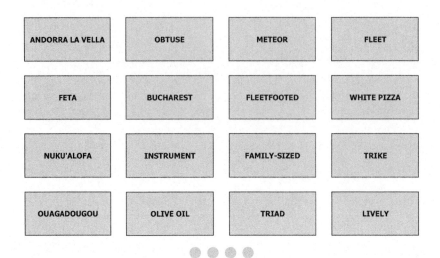

ANDORRA LA VELLA	OBTUSE	METEOR	FLEET
FETA	BUCHAREST	FLEETFOOTED	WHITE PIZZA
NUKU'ALOFA	INSTRUMENT	FAMILY-SIZED	TRIKE
OUAGADOUGOU	OLIVE OIL	TRIAD	LIVELY

Four groups of four words that share something in common :

Group #1 : _____

_____   _____   _____   _____

Group #2 : _____

_____   _____   _____   _____

Group #3 : _____

_____   _____   _____   _____

Group #4 : _____

_____   _____   _____   _____

Puzzle # 184

The solution is on page # 243

PLUTO	BOWL	GOOSE	GAIETY
STEW	ELARA	CARPO	LAUGH
MERRIMENT	BURRITO	WAFER	AMUSEMENT
SLUG	ARACHNID	VENUS	PIGEON

● ● ● ●

Four groups of four words that share something in common :

Group #1 : _____

_____ _____ _____ _____

Group #2 : _____

_____ _____ _____ _____

Group #3 : _____

_____ _____ _____ _____

Group #4 : _____

_____ _____ _____ _____

189

Puzzle # 185

The solution is on page # 243

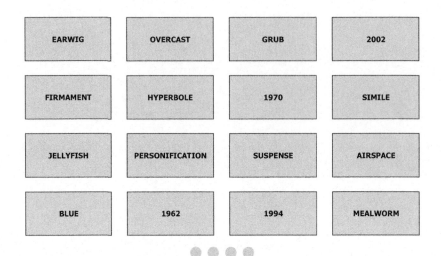

EARWIG	OVERCAST	GRUB	2002
FIRMAMENT	HYPERBOLE	1970	SIMILE
JELLYFISH	PERSONIFICATION	SUSPENSE	AIRSPACE
BLUE	1962	1994	MEALWORM

Four groups of four words that share something in common :

Group #1 : _____

_____   _____   _____   _____

Group #2 : _____

_____   _____   _____   _____

Group #3 : _____

_____   _____   _____   _____

Group #4 : _____

_____   _____   _____   _____

Puzzle # 186

The solution is on page # 244

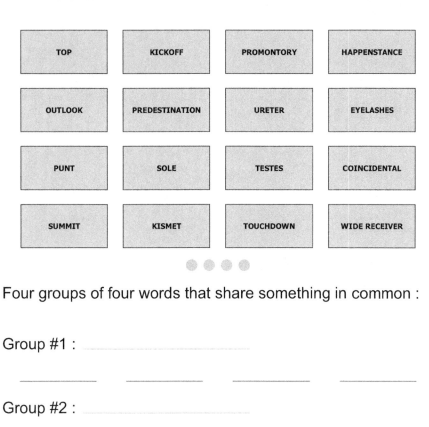

TOP	KICKOFF	PROMONTORY	HAPPENSTANCE
OUTLOOK	PREDESTINATION	URETER	EYELASHES
PUNT	SOLE	TESTES	COINCIDENTAL
SUMMIT	KISMET	TOUCHDOWN	WIDE RECEIVER

Four groups of four words that share something in common :

Group #1 : _____

_____ _____ _____ _____

Group #2 : _____

_____ _____ _____ _____

Group #3 : _____

_____ _____ _____ _____

Group #4 : _____

_____ _____ _____ _____

Puzzle # 187

The solution is on page # 244

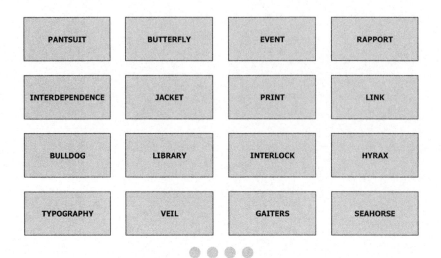

Four groups of four words that share something in common :

Group #1 : _____

_____ _____ _____ _____

Group #2 : _____

_____ _____ _____ _____

Group #3 : _____

_____ _____ _____ _____

Group #4 : _____

_____ _____ _____ _____

Puzzle # 188

The solution is on page # 244

FORTUNATE	GORGEOUS	BREASTSTROKE	INCANDESCENCE
FREESTYLE	ABLAZE	TSONGA	LIFEGUARD
RESPLENDISH	PUNJABI	PLENTIFUL	ASSAMESE
KYRGYZ	GOGGLES	GLOWING	LEGENDARY

● ● ● ●

Four groups of four words that share something in common :

Group #1 : _____

_____ _____ _____ _____

Group #2 : _____

_____ _____ _____ _____

Group #3 : _____

_____ _____ _____ _____

Group #4 : _____

_____ _____ _____ _____

Puzzle # 189

The solution is on page # 244

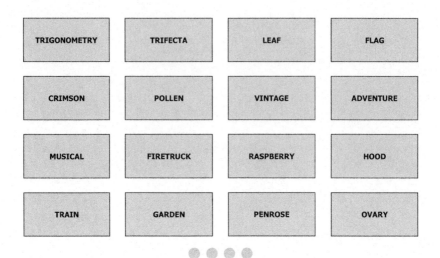

TRIGONOMETRY	TRIFECTA	LEAF	FLAG
CRIMSON	POLLEN	VINTAGE	ADVENTURE
MUSICAL	FIRETRUCK	RASPBERRY	HOOD
TRAIN	GARDEN	PENROSE	OVARY

Four groups of four words that share something in common :

Group #1 : _____

_____ _____ _____ _____

Group #2 : _____

_____ _____ _____ _____

Group #3 : _____

_____ _____ _____ _____

Group #4 : _____

_____ _____ _____ _____

Puzzle # 190

The solution is on page # 244

INESCAPABLE	CHUTE	JUMP	IMMANENT
MAGNITUDE	INDEPENDENCEDAY	THANKSGIVING	APOGEE
ALTITUDE	ALL-PERMEATING	WINDSOCK	APRIL
BOLOMETER	FEBRUARY	PHASE	EVERLASTING

Four groups of four words that share something in common :

Group #1 : _____

_____ _____ _____ _____

Group #2 : _____

_____ _____ _____ _____

Group #3 : _____

_____ _____ _____ _____

Group #4 : _____

_____ _____ _____ _____

Puzzle # 191

The solution is on page # 245

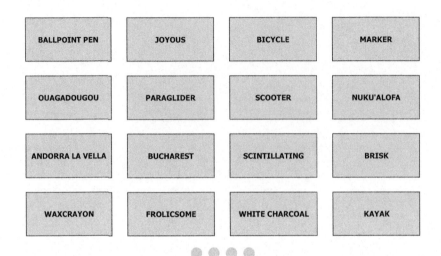

BALLPOINT PEN	JOYOUS	BICYCLE	MARKER
OUAGADOUGOU	PARAGLIDER	SCOOTER	NUKU'ALOFA
ANDORRA LA VELLA	BUCHAREST	SCINTILLATING	BRISK
WAXCRAYON	FROLICSOME	WHITE CHARCOAL	KAYAK

Four groups of four words that share something in common :

Group #1 : _____

_____ _____ _____ _____

Group #2 : _____

_____ _____ _____ _____

Group #3 : _____

_____ _____ _____ _____

Group #4 : _____

_____ _____ _____ _____

196

Puzzle # 192

The solution is on page # 245

CONCRETE	DREAMINESS	QUARTZ	BRICK
NIGHTMARE	CEILING	TRILL	HEMATITE
FANTASIA	DREAMSCAPE	CORNET	UKULELE
CUPBOARD	TABLA	STAIRCASE	CARPORT

● ● ● ●

Four groups of four words that share something in common :

Group #1 : _____

_____ _____ _____ _____

Group #2 : _____

_____ _____ _____ _____

Group #3 : _____

_____ _____ _____ _____

Group #4 : _____

_____ _____ _____ _____

Puzzle # 193

The solution is on page # 245

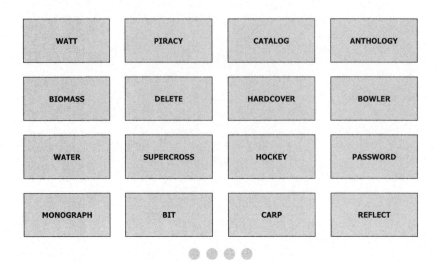

Four groups of four words that share something in common :

Group #1 : _____

_____ _____ _____ _____

Group #2 : _____

_____ _____ _____ _____

Group #3 : _____

_____ _____ _____ _____

Group #4 : _____

_____ _____ _____ _____

Puzzle # 194

The solution is on page # 245

MONOTREME	ERMINE	SWEET LIME	YUZU
MONTEREY JACK	KHASIPAPEDA	ROQUEFORT	ACTION
BUSINESS	QUESO FRESCO	POMELO	JOCOSITY
NUMBAT	TRASHSPORT	CHEESEMONGER	EARTHWORM

Four groups of four words that share something in common :

Group #1 : _____

_____ _____ _____ _____

Group #2 : _____

_____ _____ _____ _____

Group #3 : _____

_____ _____ _____ _____

Group #4 : _____

_____ _____ _____ _____

Puzzle # 195

The solution is on page # 245

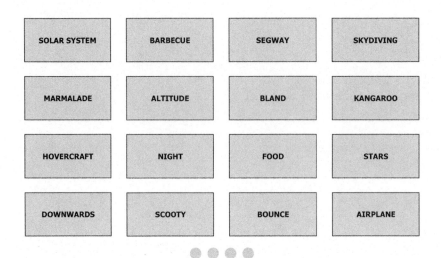

SOLAR SYSTEM	BARBECUE	SEGWAY	SKYDIVING
MARMALADE	ALTITUDE	BLAND	KANGAROO
HOVERCRAFT	NIGHT	FOOD	STARS
DOWNWARDS	SCOOTY	BOUNCE	AIRPLANE

Four groups of four words that share something in common :

Group #1 : _____

_____ _____ _____ _____

Group #2 : _____

_____ _____ _____ _____

Group #3 : _____

_____ _____ _____ _____

Group #4 : _____

_____ _____ _____ _____

200

Puzzle # 196

The solution is on page # 246

HERRING	NOIR	GLACIER	MONOCHROME
PANTHER	TUXEDO	RAY	SPEEDING
ALTERNATING	SOUND	UNPARALLELED	CREEK
FORD	DOGFISH	MODEL	STREAM

● ● ● ●

Four groups of four words that share something in common :

Group #1 : _____

_____ _____ _____ _____

Group #2 : _____

_____ _____ _____ _____

Group #3 : _____

_____ _____ _____ _____

Group #4 : _____

_____ _____ _____ _____

201

Puzzle # 197

The solution is on page # 246

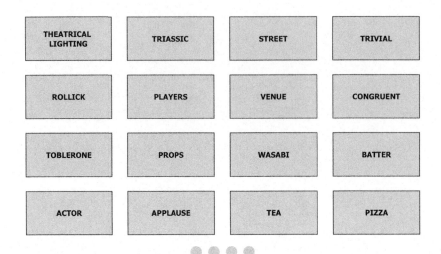

THEATRICAL LIGHTING	TRIASSIC	STREET	TRIVIAL
ROLLICK	PLAYERS	VENUE	CONGRUENT
TOBLERONE	PROPS	WASABI	BATTER
ACTOR	APPLAUSE	TEA	PIZZA

Four groups of four words that share something in common :

Group #1 : _____

_____   _____   _____   _____

Group #2 : _____

_____   _____   _____   _____

Group #3 : _____

_____   _____   _____   _____

Group #4 : _____

_____   _____   _____   _____

Puzzle # 198

The solution is on page # 246

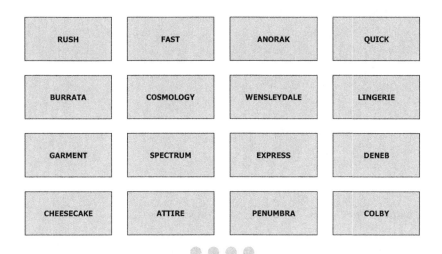

RUSH | FAST | ANORAK | QUICK

BURRATA | COSMOLOGY | WENSLEYDALE | LINGERIE

GARMENT | SPECTRUM | EXPRESS | DENEB

CHEESECAKE | ATTIRE | PENUMBRA | COLBY

Four groups of four words that share something in common :

Group #1 : _____

_____   _____   _____   _____

Group #2 : _____

_____   _____   _____   _____

Group #3 : _____

_____   _____   _____   _____

Group #4 : _____

_____   _____   _____   _____

Puzzle # 199

The solution is on page # 246

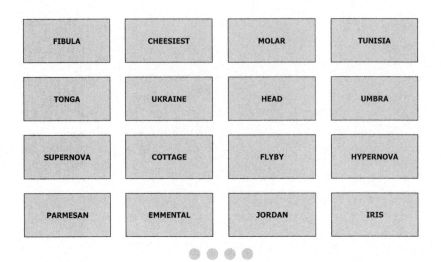

Four groups of four words that share something in common :

Group #1 : _____

_____ _____ _____ _____

Group #2 : _____

_____ _____ _____ _____

Group #3 : _____

_____ _____ _____ _____

Group #4 : _____

_____ _____ _____ _____

Puzzle # 200

The solution is on page # 246

LIGHT	DOORWAY	TEEHEE	HELMET
GLEE	WIG	VUVUZELA	ANDANTINO
BOW	COMEDY	GARTERS	GABLE
GARDEN	TUTU	HARMONICS	SNIGGER

● ● ● ●

Four groups of four words that share something in common :

Group #1 : _____

_____   _____   _____   _____

Group #2 : _____

_____   _____   _____   _____

Group #3 : _____

_____   _____   _____   _____

Group #4 : _____

_____   _____   _____   _____

205

Solutions

Puzzle #1

TRANSPORT :	VINTAGE, TRAIN, HOOD, ADVENTURE
PIZZA :	HAWAIIAN, MARGHERITA, PARMESAN, DELIVERY
FAMOUS LANDMARKS :	SAGRADA FAMILIA, TAJ MAHAL, BRANDENBURG GATE, THE LOUVRE
NIGHT :	PEACEFUL, TENEBROUS, CRICKETS, HUSH

Puzzle #2

PIZZA :	STROMBOLI, BBQ CHICKEN, THICK CRUST, SAUSAGE
FOOD :	SALSA, SUNDAE, DISH, KUMQUAT
ELEVATION :	OVERLOOK, PRECIPICE, PINNACLE, PEAK
SPORTS :	CURLING, ARCHER, BOAST, MODELS

Puzzle #3

PHONE :	CELLPHONE, TOUCH ID, VOICE ASSISTANT, DO NOT DISTURB
LOVE :	INFATUATION, FEELING, COURTSHIP, CONNECTION
CLOTHING :	HOUSECOAT, KILT, CULOTTES, KERCHIEF
JOURNEY :	ADVANCEMENT, VOYAGE, TOURING, QUEST

Puzzle #4

AMERICAN FOOTBALL :	QUARTERBACK, LINEBACKER, END ZONE, RUNNING BACK
PERSPICACIOUS :	PRUDENT, OBSERVANT, PENETRATING, LOGICAL
NATURE :	TREES, WATERFALL, GRASSLANDS, VOLCANO
SOLAR SYSTEM :	MEGACLITE, ERIS, PSYCHE, EROS

Puzzle #5

CAPITAL :	N'DJAMENA, NICOSIA, MINSK, OTTAWA
PERSPICACIOUS :	WISE, INTUITIVE, SAGACIOUS, REASONABLE
ANIMALS :	TADPOLE, TUNA, ANTEATER, BEETLE
COUNTRIES :	HONDURAS, BENIN, JAPAN, PARAGUAY

Puzzle #6

OCEAN :	OCEANIC, UNDERWATER, TREASURE, SEAWEED
ANIMALS :	GOOSE, SLUG, PIGEON, ARACHNID
SPORTS :	TIMER, TACTICAL, GEOCACHING, DRIBBLE
DRAWING INSTRUMENTS :	INKBRUSH, FELTTIPPEN, OILPASTEL, CHALK

Puzzle #7

FICTION :	LITERARY CANON, CLASSIC, STORY, PLOT TWIST
ENERGY :	EFFICIENCY, GOBY, BIOMASS, TURBINE
COLORS :	COPPER, CELADON, INDIGO, MUSTARD
EMOTION :	SYMPATHY, COMPASSION, PRIDE, INDIFFERENCE

Puzzle #8

SHUTTER :	PANORAMA, EXPOSURE, DEPTH OF FIELD, PORTRAIT
FOOD :	SQUASH, TURMERIC, LADLE, SPAGHETTI
CAPITAL :	VIENTIANE, CASTRIES, VICTORIA, WARSAW
WEATHER :	DEGREE, EYE, SURGE, GRAUPEL

Puzzle #9

EPHEMERAL :	INTERMITTENT, INCIDENTAL, FLEETING, SHORT-SPOKEN
SERENDIPITY :	OPPORTUNE, UNFORESEEN, UNPREDICTABLE, DESTINY
OBJECT'S PHYSICAL SIZE :	THIN, CURVY, TINY, SHORT
LOVE :	HAPPINESS, ROMANCE, ATTRACTION, SENTIMENT

Puzzle #10

LITERARY :	DICTION, ARCHETYPE, PLOT, RESOLUTION
COLORS :	EMERALD, JET, PEACH, WISTERIA
HUMOR :	GIGGLE, CACKLE, CHUCKLE, MIRTH
BODY :	IRIS, FIBULA, HEAD, MOLAR

Puzzle #11

COLOR RED :	STOPSIGN, REDWINE, RUBYGEMSTONE, APPLE
PARACHUTE :	CANOPY, PARATROOPER, LANDING, SKYDIVING
PERSPICACIOUS :	SHARP-WITTED, COGNIZANT, GENIUS, CANNY
SPORTS :	TELEGAMING, TRIATHLON, CYCLING, FIA

Puzzle #12

HARD MATERIALS :	GARNET, SERPENTINE, FLINT, CONCRETE
FICTION :	IMAGINATION, PAGE-TURNER, CLIMAX, SETTING
ART :	QUILL, DRAWING, CRAFT, CARVE
HOUSE :	GUTTERS, SHELVES, LINTEL, NEWEL

Puzzle #13

FOOD :	POPOVERS, MAIZE, MINT, SUNFLOWER
CINEMA :	REEL, SOUNDTRACK, AUDIENCE, FILM
SPORTS :	BEST, ESPORTS, DISCIPLINE, PHYSICAL
POSITIVE WORDS :	IMAGINE, VIGOROUS, STIRRING, GENUINE

Puzzle #14

PERSPICACIOUS :	ASTUTE, CLEAR-SIGHTED, INFORMED, JUDICIOUS
TRANSPORTATION :	YACHT, CANOE, CRUISESHIP, SUBMARINE
PIZZA :	TAKEOUT, BRICK OVEN, DEEP-DISH, MUSHROOM
OBFUSCATE :	DISTORT, PERPLEXITY, FOG, CONFUSION

Puzzle #15

SEASONS :	SPRING, FALL, WINTER, SUMMER
WHEELS :	SAILBOAT, SUBWAY, BICYCLE, RICKSHAW
SPORTS :	SHOOT, SURGE, OFFSIDES, SPORTSBOOK
CINEMA :	REEL, SOUNDTRACK, AUDIENCE, FILM

Puzzle #16

FOOD :	PARSNIP, ASPARAGUS, DRESSING, FRUIT
OBFUSCATE :	MYSTIFICATION, CLOUD, KOWTOW, SAGACIOUS
NIGHT :	SKY, CANDLELIGHT, HOOT, STARS
UBIQUITOUS :	INESCAPABLE, ALL-PERMEATING, IMMANENT, EVERLASTING

Puzzle #17

CAPITAL :	KHARTOUM, HAVANA, BEIRUT, BISSAU
SESQUIPEDALIAN :	OSTENTATIOUS, REDUNDANT, COMPLICATED, DISCURSIVE
PLANTS :	STYLE, GRASS, PALMATE, PALM
STARS :	COSMIC, SOLAR, URSA MAJOR, ASTRAL

Puzzle #18

CAPITAL :	NAYPYIDAW, KUWAIT CITY, FUNAFUTI, BELMOPAN
INSECTS :	SILVERFISH, BUTTERFLY, ANT, GREEN LACEWING
CONSERVATION :	CONSERVATIONIST, HERPETOLOGY, REPTILE, MARINE
PARACHUTE :	HARNESS, DEPLOYMENT, TANDEM, DESCENT

Puzzle #19

COLORS :	SILVER, RAINBOW, SCARLET, DENIM
SERENDIPITY :	HAZARDS, PROVIDENCE, KARMA, UNFORESEEN
WEATHER :	UPWELLING, TEMPERATE, ZONE, RAIN
FOOD :	COCONUT, MENU, SPATULA, CITRUS

Puzzle #20

TECHNOLOGY :	TECH ECOSYSTEM, COMMUNICATION, TECH INDUSTRY, ADVANCEMENT
CAPITAL :	BAKU, ASUNCIÓN, LONDON, NAIROBI
EFFERVESCENT :	IRREPRESSIBLE, MERRY, JUBILANT, EBULLIENT
TRIANGLE :	THEOREM, TRAFFIC, PENROSE, GEOMETRY

Puzzle #21

SERENDIPITY :	OPPORTUNE, UNFORESEEN, UNPREDICTABLE, DESTINY
CIRCULAR OBJECTS :	PIE, RECORD, BADGE, TIRES
SPEED :	LIGHTFOOTED, INSTANTANEOUS, NIMBLE, BREAKNECK
PHOTOGRAPHY :	VIEWFINDER, PORTRAIT, TRIPOD, EXPOSURE

Puzzle #22

CALENDAR :	NIGHT, NEWYEARSDAY, AUGUST, AFTERNOON
MANGA :	SAMURAI, DRAMA, SEINEN, MECHA
FOOD :	RECIPE, MUNCH, RICE, CASSAVA
FICTION :	IMAGINATION, PAGE-TURNER, CLIMAX, SETTING

Puzzle #23

POSITIVE WORDS :	BUBBLY, FAVORABLE, LUMINOUS, ADORABLE
DREAM :	DREAMLIKE, DREAMT, GOAL, ASPIRATION
FOOD :	BACON, TARRAGON, PORK, NUT
TIME :	AGE, DURATION, PAST, SECONDS

Puzzle #24

CAPITAL :	N'DJAMENA, NICOSIA, MINSK, OTTAWA
COLORS :	ECRU, APRICOT, VIRIDIAN, LIME
FISH :	ANCHOVY, ENERGY, DAM, CARBON
TOMATO :	CAPRESE, SAUTÉED, SOLANUM LYCOPERSICUM, JUICE

Puzzle #25

SKY :	NEBULA, OUTER SPACE, STARRY, SUN
ANIMALS :	BEAR, TURKEY, LADYBUG, PARAKEET
EMOTION :	EUPHORIA, DESPERATION, CONTEMPT, JEALOUSY
MUSICAL INSTRUMENTS :	SITAR, VIOLIN, TAMBOURINE, DRUMS

Puzzle #26

MUSIC :	ARIOSO, MALLETS, FORTE, TONIC
ASTRONOMY :	CORONA, WANING, RADIANT, COMET
ART :	BRUSH, INK, CONTRAST, DECORATE
FISH :	HALIBUT, WALLEYE, ICEFISH, PERCH

Puzzle #27

PETS :	CANARY, PARROT, BETTAFISH, AXOLOTL
TOMATO :	ROMA, BRUSCHETTA, JUICY, SUN-DRIED
GREEN :	KERMIT, GREENHOUSE, CONSERVATION, EVERGREEN
PERSPICACIOUS :	ASTUTE, CLEAR-SIGHTED, INFORMED, JUDICIOUS

Puzzle #28

COMPUTERS :	KERNEL, TAG, DATA, FIRMWARE
WEATHER :	SQUALL, STRATUS, FOG, WEDGE
FICTION :	IMAGINATION, PAGE-TURNER, CLIMAX, SETTING
FOOD :	CHOCOLATE, TOMATO, SORBET, BROWNIE

Puzzle #29

POSITIVE WORDS :	NURTURING, CONSTANT, CREATIVE, POPULAR
SPORTS :	CREW, DEFENCE, CASUAL, SPAR
COUNTRIES :	AUSTRIA, LIBERIA, BELIZE, POLAND
MUSIC :	CYMBALS, CONCH, GRAVE, SCHERZO

Puzzle #30

TRAVELING ON FOOT :	PLOD, TRAIPSE, PROMENADE, LURCH
CONSERVATION :	CONSERVATIONIST, HERPETOLOGY, REPTILE, MARINE
HOLIDAYS :	NEW YEAR'S, THANKSGIVING, CHRISTMAS, HALLOWEEN
POSITIVE WORDS :	WHOLESOME, CHAMP, LOVELY, BRILLIANT

Puzzle #31

CAPITAL :	VALLETTA, ASMARA, LUANDA, SARAJEVO
CLOTHING :	TIGHTS, GOWN, NIGHTGOWN, UMBRELLA
FOOD :	GRANOLA, PUDDING, LOQUAT, SOUR
SPORTS :	COMBAT, DODGEBALL, OUTSPORT, DEFICIT

Puzzle #32

HARD MATERIALS :	MARBLE, ALUMINA, METEORITE, PUMICE
OCEAN :	LIGHTHOUSE, SURF, BEACHCOMBING, PIRATE
DOGS :	BASENJI, HOUND, RETRIEVER, MASTIFF
ANIMALS :	MANTIS, BISON, IMPALA, WHELK

Puzzle #33

COMPUTERS :	TOOLBAR, PIRATE, UNIX, KEYBOARD
QUIXOTIC :	VISIONARY, WHIMSICAL, QUIXOTIC, UTOPIA
FISH :	COD, OARFISH, RADIATE, MEGALODON
PLANTS :	MERISTEM, EVERGREEN, CACTUS, HASTATE

Puzzle #34

DREAM :	ILLUSION, DREAMING, REVERIE, VISION
COUNTRIES :	GABON, IRAN, GUINEA, FIJI
EFFULGENT :	RESPLENDENT, EXUBERANCE, GLISTERING, GLARE
BODIES OF WATER :	TRIBUTARY, SWAMP, BOG, MARSH

Puzzle #35

COLORS :	BUFF, PALE, SLATE, KHAKI
CIRCULAR OBJECTS :	TARGET, BUBBLE, BAGEL, BUTTON
TRANSPORT :	ABS, ACCESSORIES, SHIFT, ALLOYS
MAMMALS :	POLARBEAR, CHEETAH, KOALA, OCELOT

Puzzle #36

PLANTS :	POLLINATE, EPICOTYL, BERRY, INTERNODE
SEATING ARRANGEMENTS :	MASSAGE CHAIR, DAYBED, STOOL, PICNICTABLE
ART :	PASTEL, SOLVENT, PENCIL, MOSAIC
SUN :	SUNBURNED, SUNNIEST, SUNKEN, SUNTRAP

Puzzle #37

ANIMALS :	GROUSE, NUTHATCH, FLAMINGO, PELICAN
FOOD :	VEAL, YAM, MINTS, LIVER
SPORTS :	OCCUPATION, DISCUS, PARALYMPIC, COMPETITOR
HARD MATERIALS :	EMERALD, SHALE, DIAMOND, GLASS

Puzzle #38

CONSERVATION :	INSECT, CAMOUFLAGE, ENDANGERED, PRESERVATION
ANIMALS :	LLAMA, FISH, MOSQUITO, DUCK
PIZZA :	PROSCIUTTO, SAUCE, PIZZERIA, BASIL
BOOK :	STORY, E-BOOK, BESTSELLER, COMPETITION

Puzzle #39

EFFULGENT :	VIVID, EFFERVESCENT, RADIANCE, PHOSPHORESCENT
ELEVATION :	HEIGHT, HILL, SUMMIT BID, SKYLINE
OBFUSCATE :	FOG, GARRULOUS, OPAQUE, BLUR
ASTRONOMY :	DENSITY, VENUS, MIR, MERCURY

Puzzle #40

BLACK :	BLACKMAIL, BLACK BELT, MELANIN, ONYX
SPORTS :	SKI, DROP, COACHES, HOBBY
FOOD :	SOYBEANS, LASAGNA, TOFFEE, COOKIE
FICTION :	DYSTOPIA, CHARACTER, BESTSELLER, IMAGINARY

Puzzle #41

SWIMMING :	TRAINING, STROKE, SWIM LESSON, LANE
FISH :	ANCHOVY, ENERGY, DAM, CARBON
ART :	ARTISTIC, ABSTRACT, CRITIQUE, GILDING
SPORTS :	FLIP, GYM, WRESTLING, FOOTBALLER

Puzzle #42

FOOD :	HONEY, GRAIN, ROSEMARY, SOUP
PHILATELY :	ALBUM, PERFORATION, PLATE NUMBER, PHILATELIST
UBIQUITOUS :	TOTAL, UNIVERSAL, OMNICOMPETENT, CONSTANT
FAMOUS LANDMARKS :	ST PETER'S BASILICA, SAGRADA FAMILIA, WESTMINSTER ABBEY, GREAT SPHINX

Puzzle #43

TIME :	PERIOD, FUTURE, CENTURY, SECONDS
CIRCULAR OBJECTS :	CD, DVD, BALLOON, CLOCK
GREEN :	KERMIT, GREENHOUSE, CONSERVATION, EVERGREEN
SPORTS :	SPORTFUL, DEFENSE, BOBSLEIGH, WIT

Puzzle #44

GREEN :	TEAL, SPINACH, ALPINE, LEAVES
WHEELS :	KAYAK, ZEPPELIN, UNICYCLE, SUBMARINE
CITRUS FRUITS :	BITTERLIME, NAVEL ORANGE, MICRANTHA, DJERUK LIMO
WEATHER :	LOW, INVERSION, RAINBOW, SNOWSTORM

Puzzle #45

EFFULGENT :	GLEAMING, GAIETY, JOYOUS, RADIANCE
CONSERVATION :	BIODIVERSITY, AQUATIC, RAINFOREST, TERRESTRIAL
POSITIVE WORDS :	HEAVENLY, WELCOME, FINE, ROBUST
FOOD :	ORANGE, RIBS, DOUGH, CORNMEAL

Puzzle #46

TECHNOLOGY :	TECHNOLOGICAL, AUGMENTED REALITY, AUTOMATION, TECH-SAVVY
FAMOUS LANDMARKS :	TABLE MOUNTAIN, BIG BEN, KREMLIN, COLOSSEUM
LANGUAGES :	GREEK, GAELIC, KURDISH, BERBER
FOOD :	MERINGUE, ROAST, FLAX, MUSSELS

Puzzle #47

WATER :	BECK, GULF, ICE, COVE
QUIXOTIC :	IDEALISTIC, IMPULSIVE, HOPEFUL, UNATTAINABLE
PIZZA :	TAKEOUT, BRICK OVEN, DEEP-DISH, MUSHROOM
SEASONS :	SPRING, FALL, WINTER, SUMMER

Puzzle #48

ART :	FORM, SHADE, PHOTO, TOOLS
PLANTS :	PEDUNCLE, SOIL, FOREST, SPINE
EFFULGENT :	VIVID, EFFERVESCENT, RADIANCE, PHOSPHORESCENT
POSITIVE WORDS :	INVENTIVE, AWESOME, COMPOSED, VALUED

Puzzle #49

CIRCULAR OBJECTS :	PIZZA, RECORD, TARGET, MEDAL
INSECTS :	EARWIG, PILL BUG, YELLOW JACKET, WEEVIL
TRANSPORT :	REFINEMENT, RIDE, SPORTINESS, DESIGN
PLANTS :	FERN, COROLLA, STOMA, SEEDLING

Puzzle #50

BLACK :	BLACK HOLE, ABYSS, BLACKENED, BLACKSMITH
ANIMALS :	PEAFOWL, PIKA, GAVIAL, TICK
SERENDIPITY :	WINDFALL, CIRCUMSTANCE, WINDFALL, SERENDIPITY
MUSIC :	ALPHORN, SAW, FIDDLE, ALLEGRO

Puzzle #51

FOOD :	TARO, CILANTRO, KALE, STOMACH
LANGUAGES :	XIANG, SINDHI, ZULU, BENGALI
ANIMALS :	JAY, EOHIPPUS, BASILISK, HIPPO
COUNTRIES :	TUNISIA, JORDAN, UKRAINE, TONGA

Puzzle #52

SCENIC :	STREAMS, VOLCANOES, DUNES, ISLANDS
OBJECT'S PHYSICAL SIZE :	TALL, STUBBY, FAT, MINIATURE
FOOD :	CHILI, CORN, SPUDS, SALMON
FEELINGS :	ENTHUSIASTIC, SERENE, THRILLED, HAPPY

Puzzle #53

SUN :	SUNBURNED, SUNNIEST, SUNKEN, SUNTRAP
ANIMALS :	PLOVER, SMILODON, HERON, CUTWORM
OBFUSCATE :	VICISSITUDE, MELLIFLUOUS, COMPLICATE, JUMBLE
POSITIVE WORDS :	FABULOUS, MOVING, ACCEPTED, GREEN

Puzzle #54

JOURNEY :	PASSAGE, WANDER, TRANSFER, HIKE
CAPITAL :	LUXEMBOURG CITY, DODOMA, CARACAS, ALGIERS
GEOMETRIC FIGURES :	RHOMBOID, ANNULUS, QUADRANGLE, TRAPEZOID
DOGS :	VIZSLA, GROWL, BEAGLE, GREYHOUND

Puzzle #55

EMOTIONS :	HAPPINESS, FEAR, ANGER, LOVE
COMEDY :	LAUGHTER, MISCHIEF, HUMOR, CHUCKLE
TRANSPORTATION :	TRAIN, SEGWAY, SKATEBOARD, SAILBOAT
FOOD :	LICORICE, PIE, POPSICLE, PLATE

Puzzle #56

EFFERVESCENT :	GIDDY, CHEERY, SPARKLING, ANIMATED
BODY :	PINKY, FACE, HAND, SKULL
ENERGY :	ROUGHY, SHARK, VOLTAGE, ELECTRON
WEATHER :	KELVIN, KNOT, WHITEOUT, SLEET

Puzzle #57

COMPUTERS :	NET, SPAM, TRASH, GIGABYTE
TRAVELING ON FOOT :	TIPTOE, CAPER, HOP, RAMBLE
OBFUSCATE :	PERNICIOUS, INTRANSIGENT, SESQUIPEDALIAN, CRYPTIC
ART :	GESSO, CLOISONNÉ, CHARCOAL, ERASE

Puzzle #58

MUSIC :	FOURTH, MARCATO, OCTATONIC, CIMBALOM
EFFULGENT :	ILLUMINANT, SHEEN, LUMINOUS, SCINTILLANT
STARS :	COSMIC, SOLAR, URSA MAJOR, ASTRAL
PETS :	LIZARD, POTBELLIEDPIG, MARMOSET, GUPPY

Puzzle #59

CLOTHING :	SHAWL, HOODIE, CAP, TURBAN
COUNTRIES :	JAPAN, NORWAY, ISRAEL, ESWATINI
TRANSPORT :	FLY, PRECISION, TECHNOLOGY, TIRES
CAPITAL :	SKOPJE, SEOUL, PORT-AU-PRINCE, SINGAPORE

Puzzle #60

CAPITAL :	SANA'A, SAN MARINO|, BRIDGETOWN, MANAMA
MANGA :	HAREM, HORROR, FANTASY, CYBERPUNK
MUSIC :	KAZOO, REPEAT, OBOE, ANIMATO
COMPUTERS :	DOWNLOAD, DATABASE, HOST, COPY

Puzzle #61

FAMILY :	MOTHER, FATHER, BROTHER, SISTER
TIME :	AGE, DURATION, PAST, SECONDS
CAPITAL :	N'DJAMENA, NICOSIA, MINSK, OTTAWA
CLOTHING :	SWEATER, SHOES, PEPLUM, SPACESUIT

Puzzle #62

RED :	MAHOGANY, STOP, BRICK, MAROON
HOUSE :	ENTRANCE, MAILBOX, CARPET, STAIRWAY
FOOD :	MUTTON, EDIBLE, SQUID, PICNIC
ENERGY :	AC, ELECTRICITY, CURRENT, GENERATOR

Puzzle #63

MANGA :	ACTION, ALIENS, COMICS, SUPERPOWERS
EFFULGENT :	RADIANT, BEAMING, DAZZLING, SHIMMERING
FRUIT :	CHERRY, GUAVA, HONEYDEW, CANTALOUPE
HOUSE :	SKYLIGHT, HOUSE, AWNING, ROOM

Puzzle #64

NIGHT :	SKY, CANDLELIGHT, HOOT, STARS
ANIMALS :	ROUNDWORM, LEOPARD, DIATOM, TOUCAN
COUNTRIES :	MALAWI, RUSSIA, BRAZIL, ARGENTINA
MAMMALS :	BROWNBEAR, CHIMPANZEE, ZEBRA, JAGUAR

Puzzle #65

COUNTRIES :	VENEZUELA, INDIA, TURKEY, TUVALU
DREAM :	DREAMINESS, DREAMER, AMBITION, FANTASY
MUSIC :	TREBLE, TRIANGLE, PIPA, MELODY
ANIMALS :	FLY, PEKINGESE, COD, SKUNK

Puzzle #66

HOUSE :	OVERHANG, SHOWER, BROOM, QUILT
POSITIVE WORDS :	KIND, VIVACIOUS, SUPERB, FRESH
SOLAR SYSTEM :	ANANKE, CALLISTO, TITAN, SATURN
COMEDY :	RIDICULOUS, CLOWNING, ZANY, WHIMSICAL

Puzzle #67

ANIMALS :	TERRIER, STONEFLY, NARWHAL, HEDGEHOG
LOVE :	HAPPINESS, ROMANCE, ATTRACTION, SENTIMENT
BODY :	LOBE, NOSTRIL, BUTTOCKS, ADENOIDS
OCEAN :	ISLANDS, COASTLINE, MARITIME, DIVING

Puzzle #68

SPEED :	SPRIGHTLY, AGILE, BULLET, POSTHASTE
FISH :	RADIANT, SUNLIGHT, GRID, FURNACE
FRUIT :	APPLE, MANGO, HUCKLEBERRY, APRICOT
FOOD :	DRIED, GRAVY, ARTICHOKE, GUAVA

Puzzle #69

POSITIVE WORDS :	HONEST, LUCID, ESTEEMED, REWARDING
EFFULGENT :	SPARKLING, RADIANT, EFFULGENT, EFFERVESCENT
TOMATO :	PASTE, FRUIT, RED, GRILLED
ELEVATION :	AERIAL VIEW, CLIFF, BAROMETRIC PRESSURE, OBSERVATION

Puzzle #70

SPORTS :	JOUSTING, CROSS, YOGA, CARS
CAPITAL :	ISLAMABAD, GUATEMALA CITY, KIGALI, NIAMEY
COMPUTERS :	COMMAND, DOMAIN, SCRIPT, SCREEN
ART :	FORM, SHADE, PHOTO, TOOLS

Puzzle #71

PETS :	COCKATIEL, RAT, SKUNK, SNAKE
ANIMALS :	MAMMOTH, XENOPS, HEN, JAGUAR
LANGUAGES :	ALBANIAN, TELUGU, CZECH, JAVANESE
MUSIC :	METER, CODA, KEYBOARD, SYMPHONY

Puzzle #72

HOUSE :	TOILET, POOL, WALKWAY, PORTICO
CONNECTION :	INTERDEPENDENCE, RAPPORT, LINK, INTERLOCK
JOURNEY :	ITINERARY, CROSSING, TOUR, ODYSSEY
SPORTS :	POPULAR, BOWLING, WAGGERY, GAMEDAY

Puzzle #73

ENERGY :	POWER, BATTERY, TIDAL, GRAYLING
ANIMALS :	GROUSE, NUTHATCH, FLAMINGO, PELICAN
SOLID :	RUBY, LIMESTONE, GLASS, TOPAZ
GEOMETRIC FIGURES :	HEART, ANNULUS, PENTAGON, RHOMBUS

Puzzle #74

PLETHORA :	PROFUSION, ABOUNDING, PLENITUDE, COPIOUS
BODY :	FILLING, EYEBROW, NAVEL, NECK
SHUTTER :	POLARIZER, APERTURE, FILTER, RULE OF THIRDS
CAPITAL :	KUALA LUMPUR, SANTO DOMINGO, DJIBOUTI, PYONGYANG

Puzzle #75

HOUSE :	MAT, LOCK, STAIRS, CRIB
SPORTS :	SUBMARINE, CHESS, ROWING, TRAD
BASKETBALL :	LAYUP, JUMP BALL, TIMEOUT, BUZZER BEATER
ELEVATION :	ESCARPMENT, TERRAIN, FOOTHILLS, PLATEAU

Puzzle #76

BOOK :	SCORE, RECREATION, SHELF, PUBLISHER
SPORTS :	BILLIARDS, ATHLETICS, SHOT, HOBBIES
FOOD :	COOKBOOK, BRAN, ENDIVE, YOGURT
EMOTION :	ANTICIPATION, CONFUSION, FEAR, ANXIETY

Puzzle #77

TRANSPORTATION :	HANGGLIDER, TRAIN, AIRPLANE, MOTORCYCLE
LANGUAGES :	GREEK, GAELIC, KURDISH, BERBER
WATER :	LAKE, WATERCOURSE, WATERCOURSE, WATERFALL
TECHNOLOGY :	NETWORKING, PROGRESS, INTERNET, LAPTOP

Puzzle #78

FICTION :	IMAGINATION, PAGE-TURNER, CLIMAX, SETTING
ENERGY :	COAL, RENEWABLE, STURGEON, LOACH
EPHEMERAL :	HASTY, EPHEMERAL, SHORT-LIVED, INCIDENTAL
BODY :	PINKY, FACE, HAND, SKULL

Puzzle #79

HOUSE :	ENTRY, WALL, HEATER, PAINTING
ASTRONOMY :	URANUS, SYZYGY, NASA, STAR
WEATHER :	HUMID, WINDSOCK, UPWIND, TORNADO
LITERARY :	PARADOX, MOTIF, ANECDOTE, PROTAGONIST

Puzzle #80

SEATING ARRANGEMENTS :	BARSTOOL, THRONE, FOOTSTOOL, ROCKING CHAIR
COLORS :	SALMON, SHAMROCK, SLATE, AZURE
ANIMALS :	CHIHUAHUA, DODO, BOXER, DINORNIS
QUIXOTIC :	IDEALISM, FANCIFUL, QUIXOTISM, UNREALISM

Puzzle #81

MUSIC :	ARIOSO, MALLETS, FORTE, TONIC
SOLID :	DIAMOND, ALUMINUM, CERAMIC, GNEISS
RED :	RUST, ROSE, ROUGE, VELVET
NIGHT :	OWLS, BLACKNESS, NIGHTFALL, EVENING

Puzzle #82

MUSIC :	BOW, HARMONICS, VUVUZELA, ANDANTINO
NIGHT :	INSOMNIA, NIGHTCAP, SLEEP, NIGHT SKY
PHONE :	AIRPLANE MODE, PASSWORD, CAMERA, RINGTONE
CIRCULAR OBJECTS :	MOON, PANCAKE, PIECHART, RING

Puzzle #83

TRANSPORT :	PETROL, CRUISE, ULTIMATE, MERCEDES
ANIMALS :	ELAND, NABARLEK, BASS, GIRAFFE
OBJECT'S PHYSICAL SIZE :	SLENDER, COLOSSAL, LANKY, GIANT
TRAVELING ON FOOT :	SPRINT, PACE, RUN, STROLL

Puzzle #84

TRIANGLE :	OBTUSE, TRIKE, INSTRUMENT, TRIAD
HUMOR :	HAHA, HILARIOUS, CHORTLE, WIT
HOUSE :	LAUNDRY, DOORKNOB, COUNTER, PATIO
COLORS :	COLOR, GOLDENROD, BLUE, TAN

Puzzle #85

LANGUAGES :	FRISIAN, INUKTITUT, SWEDISH, ARABIC
SKY :	HEAVEN, SPACE, AERONAUTICS, DAY
FOOD :	SALSA, SUNDAE, DISH, KUMQUAT
COUNTRIES :	SOMALIA, ARMENIA, MOLDOVA, PANAMA

Puzzle #86

TRANSPORTATION :	ROLLERSKATES, CAR, GOLFCART, ZEPPELIN
POSITIVE WORDS :	CLASSICAL, INSTANT, BEAUTIFUL, RESTORED
HARD MATERIALS :	BRICK, JASPER, RUBY, SAPPHIRE
LANGUAGES :	MADURESE, GERMAN, UZBEK, SPANISH

Puzzle #87

ANIMALS :	FLY, PEKINGESE, COD, SKUNK
SOLAR SYSTEM :	JUNO, HIMALIA, NEPTUNE, TRITON
POSITIVE WORDS :	HONEST, LUCID, ESTEEMED, REWARDING
SPORTS :	HURDLE, ADV, BACKPACK, POLO

Puzzle #88

QUIXOTIC :	ROMANTIC, IDEALIZED, IMAGINARY, CHASING WINDMILLS
BOOK :	BOOKMARK, GAME, EDITOR, NARRATOR
TRIANGLE :	PENROSE, TRIFECTA, TRIGONOMETRY, MUSICAL
ANIMALS :	BUSHBABY, MOUSE, HERRING, MANDRILL

Puzzle #89

FOOD :	SQUASH, TURMERIC, LADLE, SPAGHETTI
SPEED :	FLASH, SNAPPY, ZIPPY, TURBO
INSECTS :	CARPENTER ANT, TARANTULA, CICADA, HOUSEFLY
SOLID :	DIAMOND, ALUMINUM, CERAMIC, GNEISS

Puzzle #90

EPHEMERAL :	HASTY, INTERMITTENT, IMPERMANENT, TEMPORANEOUS
VEGETABLES :	GARLIC, BEET, SCALLION, GREENBEANS
ASTRONOMY :	VACUUM, PARALLAX, SOLAR, APERTURE
EFFULGENT :	GLISTER, EFFULGENT, BRILLIANT, LUMINOUS

Puzzle #91

LANGUAGES :	BASQUE, HMONG, TURKISH, DANISH
WATER :	LAKE, WATERCOURSE, WATERCOURSE, WATERFALL
PHONE :	EMOJI, TOUCHSCREEN, INTERNET, BLUETOOTH
DREAM :	IMAGINATION, DESIRE, DREAMER, DREAMED

Puzzle #92

FOOD :	CRUST, SHRIMP, CHOW, SOY
OBFUSCATE :	MYSTIFY, AMBIGUOUS, HAZE, DISSEMBLE
SUN :	SUNSETTING, SUNUP, SUNBATH, SUNLIT
TOMATO :	CAPRESE, SAUTÉED, SOLANUM LYCOPERSICUM, JUICE

Puzzle #93

COUNTRIES :	SAMOA, PERU, NAURU, ALGERIA
WATER :	RAIN, STREAM, HARBOR, ARROYO
POSITIVE WORDS :	FAMILIAR, OKAY, ADMIRE, DAZZLING
OBFUSCATE :	PERPLEX, DISTORT, VEIL, NADIR

Puzzle #94

MUSIC :	PICCOLO, MOLTO, RAINSTICK, CELLO
SEATING ARRANGEMENTS :	BARSTOOL, THRONE, FOOTSTOOL, ROCKING CHAIR
WEATHER :	CYCLONE, NEXRAD, HIGH, ALMANAC
PRINTED MATERIALS :	ENCYCLOPEDIA, MANUSCRIPT, THESIS, BIOGRAPHY

Puzzle #95

HUMOR :	HOHO, HUMOR, MERRYMENT, SMILE
OBJECT'S PHYSICAL SIZE :	THIN, CURVY, TINY, SHORT
ANIMALS :	MAMMOTH, XENOPS, HEN, JAGUAR
STAGE :	THEATRICAL LIGHTING, APPLAUSE, PROPS, ACTOR

Puzzle #96

SERENDIPITY :	PROPITIOUS, CHANCE, DESTINY, COINCIDENTAL
BOOK :	SCORE, RECREATION, SHELF, PUBLISHER
CINEMA :	PREMIERE, TRAILER, GENRE, SCENE
TOMATO :	TOMATILLO, PLUM, CHERRY, PICO DE GALLO

Puzzle #97

LITERARY :	ALLEGORY, TRAGEDY, DIALOGUE, TONE
ASTRONOMY :	DENSITY, VENUS, MIR, MERCURY
ANIMALS :	MOOSE, URCHIN, POLLIWOG, ANACONDA
SOLID :	GEODE, PUMICE, EMERALD, SLATE

Puzzle #98

POSITIVE WORDS :	ACTIVE, WOW, TRUTHFUL, MASTERFUL
FOOD :	CASSEROLE, SALAD, DAIKON, FIG
SPORTS :	SHOOTER, POSITION, SCHUSS, WORKING
LANGUAGES :	IBIBIO, MALTESE, ENGLISH, AFRIKAANS

Puzzle #99

COUNTRIES :	CUBA, NIGERIA, ECUADOR, LAOS
SESQUIPEDALIAN :	GRANDILOQUENT, ORATORICAL, PROLIX, CIRCUMLOCUTION
JOURNEY :	ITINERARY, CROSSING, TOUR, ODYSSEY
PIZZA :	WHITE PIZZA, OLIVE OIL, FAMILY-SIZED, FETA

Puzzle #100

PHONE :	CELLPHONE, TOUCH ID, VOICE ASSISTANT, DO NOT DISTURB
SEATING ARRANGEMENTS :	RECLINER, LOVESEAT, TUFFET, BEANBAG CHAIR
CALENDAR :	FRIDAY, SATURDAY, AUTUMN, BREAKFAST
BOOK :	MANUSCRIPT, SPORT, FAN, COMPETITION

Puzzle #101

CLOTHING :	FROCK, BOW, SLIP, BRACELET
QUIXOTIC :	CHIVALROUS, EXTRAVAGANT, ECCENTRIC, DREAMY
EPHEMERAL :	BRIEF, SHORT-TERM, RAPID, BRIEF
ELEVATION :	CREST, TREE LINE, VALLEYS, LOOKOUT

Puzzle #102

SOLAR SYSTEM :	ANANKE, CALLISTO, TITAN, SATURN
SPORTS :	CANOEING, DECATHLON, COMPETING, EXERCISE
ANIMALS :	MOA, SEALION, ONAGER, PENGUIN
LITERARY :	HUBRIS, SOLILOQUY, NOVEL, SONNET

Puzzle #103

ANIMALS :	SHREW, CAIMAN, DUGONG, CROW
COLORS :	EBONY, LAVENDER, SPECTRUM, EGGPLANT
SPORTS :	HURDLE, ADV, BACKPACK, POLO
CAPITAL :	NUKU'ALOFA, ANDORRA LA VELLA, BUCHAREST, OUAGADOUGOU

Puzzle #104

PLANTS :	KUDZU, MOSS, WHORLED, SPORE
PIZZA :	PADDLE, MARINARA, PINEAPPLE, GARLIC
ELEVATION :	GEOGRAPHIC COORDINATES, CANOPY, ELEVATION GAIN, HIGH
CLOTHING :	HOUSECOAT, KILT, CULOTTES, KERCHIEF

Puzzle #105

ANIMALS :	FOSSA, REPTILE, STARFISH, CICADA
EFFERVESCENT :	RADIANT, LIGHTHEARTED, EFFULGENT, JAUNTY
PERSPICACIOUS :	CLEVER, CALCULATING, RATIONAL, SMART
LANGUAGES :	SLOVENE, PASHTO, BHOJPURI, SUNDA

Puzzle #106

ENERGY :	ROUGHY, SHARK, VOLTAGE, ELECTRON
SPORTS :	SPORT, DISPORT, JUDO, PRACTICE
NAME :	MENTION, RECOGNITION, NOMENCLATURE, MIDDLE NAME
CLOTHING :	KIT, CARDIGAN, ZORIS, ONESIES

Puzzle #107

SPORTS :	WORLD, WORKOUT, BOUT, NORMAL
FICTION :	PARABLE, WHODUNIT, FANTASY, MYTH
PRINTED MATERIALS :	ALMANAC, MAGAZINE, AUTOBIOGRAPHY, BOOK
CAPITAL :	ADDIS ABABA, JUBA, MORONI, MALABO

Puzzle #108

EFFERVESCENT :	IRREPRESSIBLE, MERRY, JUBILANT, EBULLIENT
TRANSPORT :	REFINEMENT, RIDE, SPORTINESS, DESIGN
CLOTHING :	SUIT, GALOSHES, BREECHES, TOGA
FOOD :	HONEY, GRAIN, ROSEMARY, SOUP

Puzzle #109

HUMOR :	GAIETY, LAUGH, AMUSEMENT, MERRIMENT
FICTION :	NOVEL, AUTHORSHIP, ROMANCE, SUSPENSION OF DISBELIEF
LITERARY :	FORESHADOWING, ONOMATOPOEIA, FOIL, COMEDY
GEOMETRIC FIGURES :	ARROWHEAD, ARROWHEAD, SQUARE, NONAGON

Puzzle #110

HOUSE :	NOOK, STOVE, PLUMBING, BATHTUB
LANGUAGES :	TETUM, YIDDISH, AMHARIC, SOMALI
FICTION :	NOVEL, AUTHORSHIP, ROMANCE, SUSPENSION OF DISBELIEF
DREAM :	DREAMER, DREAMED, DREAMLIKE, DAYDREAM

Puzzle #111

SKY :	STRATUS, CELESTIAL, TROPOSPHERE, METEOROLOGY
FEELINGS :	EXHILARATED, ZESTFUL, CHARMED, EUPHORIC
SPORTS :	SUBMARINE, CHESS, ROWING, TRAD
SHUTTER :	ISO, SHUTTER SPEED, MEGAPIXELS, BRACKETING

Puzzle #112

PAINTING :	LINEN, ACRYLIC, MEDIUM, STILL LIFE
NATURE :	FOLIAGE, SEASHELLS, WIND, RIVER
INSECTS :	CENTIPEDE, SAND FLY, FLEA, JUNE BUG
WEATHER :	COLD, NORMAL, DRIZZLE, FAIR

Puzzle #113

SOLID :	JADE, IRON, CORUNDUM, SAPPHIRE
PIZZA :	TAKEOUT, OREGANO, CRISPY, PIZZAIOLO
ANIMALS :	MOOSE, URCHIN, POLLIWOG, ANACONDA
EMOTION :	CURIOSITY, RESENTMENT, LOVE, IRRITATION

Puzzle #114

SERENDIPITY :	KISMET, COINCIDENTAL, HAPPENSTANCE, PREDESTINATION
HARD MATERIALS :	PETRIFIEDWOOD, CORUNDUM, TOPAZ, BASALT
EPHEMERAL :	EPHEMERON, EON, SHORT-LIVED, TEMPORANEOUS
ANIMALS :	EORAPTOR, KUDU, ALLIGATOR, COATI

Puzzle #115

LANGUAGES :	KAZAKH, FAROESE, IRISH, FAROESE
ANIMALS :	OCTOPUS, CRANE, SPIDER, OKAPI
MANGA :	ACTION, ALIENS, COMICS, SUPERPOWERS
DREAM :	ILLUSION, DREAMING, REVERIE, VISION

Puzzle #116

SPEED :	FLASH, SNAPPY, ZIPPY, TURBO
JUMP :	LAUNCH, DIVE, TUMBLE, GRASSHOPPER
COLORS :	PURPLE, OCHER, RED, CERISE
PLANTS :	VENATION, TUBER, FOLIAGE, PLUMULE

Puzzle #117

ANIMALS :	MOOSE, URCHIN, POLLIWOG, ANACONDA
TOMATO :	GREEN, BEEFSTEAK, HEIRLOOM, SALAD
FEELINGS :	BLISSFUL, CHEERY, GLAD, RAPTUROUS
CAPITAL :	BUDAPEST, WINDHOEK, DILI, ROSEAU

Puzzle #118

OBFUSCATE :	ABERRATION, QUIXOTIC, OPAQUE, LABYRINTHINE
TRANSPORT :	NOTEWORTHY, PERFORM, AIRPLANE, ULTRA
BODIES OF WATER :	CREEK, ARM, OCEAN, OXBOW
EFFULGENT :	GLISTER, EFFULGENT, BRILLIANT, LUMINOUS

Puzzle #119

OBFUSCATE :	RECALCITRANT, OBFUSCATE, PERPLEXITY, MYSTIFY
TECHNOLOGY :	ARTIFICIAL INTELLIGENCE, SMARTPHONE, CUTTING-EDGE, SOFTWARE
FOOD :	BUNS, JULIENNE, OMNIVORE, NUTRIENT
POSITIVE WORDS :	NURTURING, CONSTANT, CREATIVE, POPULAR

Puzzle #120

BOOK :	FICTION, STADIUM, TABLE OF CONTENTS, PLOT
SKY :	SOLAR SYSTEM, STARS, ALTITUDE, NIGHT
MUSICAL INSTRUMENTS :	KALIMBA, SAXOPHONE, HURDYGURDY, BALALAIKA
ANIMALS :	GOLDFINCH, POMPANO, HORNET, CARNIVORA

Puzzle #121

HOUSE :	BLINDS, CELLAR, SHED, BARBECUE
CIRCULAR OBJECTS :	WHEEL, SPHERE, MEDAL, PLATE
GEOMETRIC FIGURES :	CHEVRON, CRESCENT, HEXAGON, DECAGON
WEATHER :	SQUALL, STRATUS, FOG, WEDGE

Puzzle #122

CITRUS FRUITS :	FINGER LIME, KABOSU, KEY LIME, KHASIPAPEDA
NIGHT :	OWLS, BLACKNESS, NIGHTFALL, EVENING
COMEDY :	SCREWBALL, EXAGGERATION, ECCENTRIC, GAG
CONNECTION :	INTERDEPENDENCE, RAPPORT, LINK, INTERLOCK

Puzzle #123

EMOTION :	GUILT, NOSTALGIA, AGITATION, GRATITUDE
HOUSE :	ENTRY, WALL, HEATER, PAINTING
PHILATELY :	POSTMARK, PHILATELIC SOCIETY, SOUVENIR SHEET, POSTAGE
PRINTED MATERIALS :	DIRECTORY, LITERARY, MANUSCRIPT, SCROLL

Puzzle #124

CLOTHING :	TROUSERS, BOOT, PARKA, ROBE
ANIMALS :	TIGER, OWL, HORSE, YAK
NIGHT :	INSOMNIA, NIGHTCAP, SLEEP, NIGHT SKY
FOOD :	OLEO, SHALLOTS, DINER, CRUNCH

Puzzle #125

CLOTHING :	OVERSHIRT, EARRINGS, CLOGS, BUCKLE
CAPITAL :	MBABANE, RIGA, DHAKA, MONTEVIDEO
COLORS :	GREEN, GOLD, RUSSET, AUBURN
TRANSPORT :	EXCELLENCE, TRANSPORT, SAFETY, FEELING

Puzzle #126

TRAVELING ON FOOT :	WALK, SAUNTER, GALLOP, JOG
CITRUS FRUITS :	CITRON, BLOOD ORANGE, PERSIANLIME, BERGAMOT
INSECTS :	GNAT, SCORPION, PRAYING MANTIS, FLEA BEETLE
OCEAN :	SHIP, SEAGULLS, NAUTICAL, SEASHELLS

Puzzle #127

TRANSPORT :	NOTEWORTHY, PERFORM, AIRPLANE, ULTRA
MUSIC :	SONATA, MUTE, SEQUENCE, DULCIMER
STARS :	ASTRONOMER, INTERSTELLAR, LUMINOUS, PULSAR
LANGUAGES :	PERSIAN, HAUSA, ROMANIAN, SAMI

Puzzle #128

FISH :	WINDMILL, RESERVOIR, TRANSMIT, GUPPY
FOOD :	ANISE, FENNEL, TANGERINE, CAVIAR
SPORTS :	MOTORCYCLE, TRAINING, COMPETES, HANDBALL
ANIMALS :	SHRIMP, IGUANA, CRICKET, ANGONOKA

Puzzle #129

RED :	SUNSET, MAHOGANY, POPPY, RUBY
CHEESE :	CHEVRE, JARLSBERG, BLUE, FETA
SCENIC :	VALLEYS, HILLS, PLAINS, SCENIC
BLACK :	BLACK HOLE, ABYSS, BLACKENED, BLACKSMITH

Puzzle #130

COUNTRIES :	ANGOLA, MALDIVES, YEMEN, LIBYA
CLOTHING :	LAPEL, SHIRT, UNDERWEAR, COSTUME
TRANSPORT :	TRANSIT, BOOST, SPORTSTER, EXPENSIVE
CONNECTION :	INTEGRATION, INTERCONNECTION, NEXUS, BRIDGE

Puzzle #131

COUNTRIES :	VIETNAM, NICARAGUA, ITALY, DENMARK
MYTHICAL CREATURES :	GRIFFIN, UNICORN, DRAGON, PHOENIX
MAMMALS :	FOX, LEOPARD, ELEPHANT, GIRAFFE
ANIMALS :	PLANKTON, TANAGER, BARNACLE, MINK

Puzzle #132

BODY :	TARSAL, LEG, BREAST, CELL
RED :	FOXY, APPLE, RUST, BRICK
EMOTION :	SHAME, HAPPINESS, AFFECTION, SADNESS
VEGETABLES :	JICAMA, RADISH, SWEETPOTATO, SPINACH

Puzzle #133

JOURNEY :	EXPEDITION, MIGRATION, SAFARI, SOJOURN
COMPUTERS :	BUFFER, SPYWARE, PATH, SERVER
CLOTHING :	BUTTON, DIRNDL, SANDALS, FEDORA
FEELINGS :	VIVACIOUS, JOYFUL, ELATED, PLEASED

Puzzle #134

ANIMALS :	ELAND, NABARLEK, BASS, GIRAFFE
CONSERVATION :	RESTORATION, ECOSYSTEM, EXTINCTION, MIGRATION
LANGUAGES :	MADURESE, GERMAN, UZBEK, SPANISH
INSECTS :	CATERPILLAR, KATYDID, DRAGONFLY, MIDGE

Puzzle #135

CLOTHING :	SARONG, LOAFERS, HAT, SLACKS
JUMP :	POLE VAULT, HIGH JUMP, HIGH-FLYING, PARKOUR
SPEED :	HEADLONG, RAPID, QUICKENED, SPEEDY
COUNTRIES :	LEBANON, ANDORRA, FRANCE, CHAD

Puzzle #136

OBFUSCATE :	MISLEAD, COVER, TRUCULENT, SCREEN
PLANTS :	BEAN, NECTAR, NETTED, SHAMROCK
UBIQUITOUS :	PERENNIAL, PERVADING, TOTAL, ALL-AROUND
CLOTHING :	KIMONO, FEZ, SNEAKERS, CLOAK

Puzzle #137

BLACK :	CHARCOAL, SHADOW, STEALTH, BLACKENED CHICKEN
VEGETABLES :	GARLIC, BEET, SCALLION, GREENBEANS
PLANTS :	RINGS, HERB, CORK, SEPAL
FOOD :	PLATTER, QUINOA, SPICES, GYRO

Puzzle #138

ANIMALS :	CHIPMUNK, NAUTILUS, CHEETAH, MUSKRAT
PHONE :	EMOJI, TOUCHSCREEN, INTERNET, BLUETOOTH
EMOTION :	COMPASSION, FRUSTRATION, DEVOTION, ANGER
COMPUTERS :	FONT, MONITOR, SAVE, PLATFORM

Puzzle #139

LANGUAGES :	FRENCH, DUTCH, SOTHO, BULGARIAN
MANGA :	ROMANCE, MANGAKA, ECCHI, OTAKU
COLORS :	PRIMARY, CHARCOAL, CREAM, AMBER
FISH :	COAL, SNAPPER, VIPERFISH, HYDROGEN

Puzzle #140

FRUIT :	CHERRY, GUAVA, HONEYDEW, CANTALOUPE
CLOTHING :	SWEATER, SHOES, PEPLUM, SPACESUIT
PERSPICACIOUS :	SHREWD, RATIONAL, DISCERNING, DISCRIMINATING
ANIMALS :	COBRA, FIREANT, ISOPOD, PANGOLIN

Puzzle #141

LITERARY :	FORESHADOWING, ONOMATOPOEIA, FOIL, COMEDY
SPORTS :	MODEL, OUTCLASS, DIVERSION, BAT
COUNTRIES :	DJIBOUTI, SURINAME, GEORGIA, BELGIUM
CAPITAL :	ISLAMABAD, GUATEMALA CITY, KIGALI, NIAMEY

Puzzle #142

LANGUAGES :	NORWEGIAN, FILIPINO, TAMIL, MAORI
ANIMALS :	PEAFOWL, PIKA, GAVIAL, TICK
SPORTS :	LIMITED, SUBBUTEO, SPORTER, OFFSIDE
CALENDAR :	CHRISTMAS, MAY, JANUARY, SEPTEMBER

Puzzle #143

CAPITAL :	SKOPJE, SEOUL, PORT-AU-PRINCE, SINGAPORE
OBJECT'S PHYSICAL SIZE :	LEAN, BULKY, DELICATE, ENORMOUS
FICTION :	ADVENTURE, WORLD-BUILDING, RESOLUTION, FABLE
TRIANGLE :	EQUILATERAL, TRIANGULAR, SCALENE, SHAPE

Puzzle #144

COLOR RED :	REDTULIP, STRAWBERRY, FIRETRUCK, CHERRY
BODIES OF WATER :	CREEK, ARM, OCEAN, OXBOW
MUSICAL INSTRUMENTS :	OBOE, PIANO, TRUMPET, GLOCKENSPIEL
EFFULGENT :	SPARKLING, RADIANT, EFFULGENT, EFFERVESCENT

Puzzle #145

CAPITAL :	CONAKRY, BERN, TRIPOLI, NEW DELHI
WATER :	SOUND, GLACIER, CREEK, STREAM
CITRUS FRUITS :	LIME, DESERT LIME, RANGPURLIME, GRAPEFRUIT
FOOD :	BUTTER, HOT, MINCEMEAT, NIBBLE

Puzzle #146

SERENDIPITY :	FORTUITY, FORTUNATE, QUIRK, HAPPENSTANCE
MUSIC :	TABLA, UKULELE, CORNET, TRILL
TRANSPORTATION :	HANGGLIDER, TRAIN, AIRPLANE, MOTORCYCLE
SPORTS :	NONGAME, PREMIUM, SOCIAL, PASTIME

Puzzle #147

COLORS :	ECRU, APRICOT, VIRIDIAN, LIME
WATER :	ARM, RAPIDS, RIVER, RAPIDS
FOOD :	PASTA, PAN, COBBLER, GARLIC
PAINTING :	VARNISH, WATERCOLOR, PIGMENT, GESSO

Puzzle #148

BOOK :	SCORE, RECREATION, SHELF, PUBLISHER
ANIMALS :	WEASEL, EDENTA, TURTLE, TORTOISE
ELEVATION :	GEOGRAPHIC COORDINATES, CANOPY, ELEVATION GAIN, HIGH
COUNTRIES :	CAMEROON, MALAYSIA, USA, BOTSWANA

Puzzle #149

PETS :	BEARDEDDRAGON, BETAFISH, MACAW, GUINEAPIG
COMPUTERS :	CONFIGURE, MODEM, USERNAME, OFFLINE
BODY :	TISSUE, ANUS, TEETH, SHOULDER
COMEDY :	PRANK, LIGHTHEARTED, STAND-UP, AMUSING

Puzzle #150

LANGUAGES :	QUECHUA, ITALIAN, MACEDONIAN, YUE
CHEESE :	CHEESINESS, CHEESE DIP, CAMEMBERT, PROVOLONE
MUSIC :	PESANTE, BASS, OVERTONE, VIOLIN
COMEDY :	SCREWBALL, EXAGGERATION, ECCENTRIC, GAG

Puzzle #151

EPHEMERAL :	CEASING, MOMENTANEOUS, MOMENTARY, FITFUL
SPORTS :	ROLLICK, STREET, PLAYERS, VENUE
TRANSPORT :	FUTURISTIC, AC, TICKET, GO
CHEESE :	RICOTTA, SWISS, RED LEICESTER, CHEESECLOTH

Puzzle #152

SOLAR SYSTEM :	URANUS, KALYKE, LEDA, METIS
FOOD :	MUTTON, EDIBLE, SQUID, PICNIC
ANIMALS :	LYNX, SNAKE, SHARK, COYPU
TRAVELING ON FOOT :	CLIMB, PARADE, TREK, WHIRL

Puzzle #153

FOOD :	MARMALADE, BARBECUE, FOOD, BLAND
CAPITAL :	NUKU'ALOFA, ANDORRA LA VELLA, BUCHAREST, OUAGADOUGOU
MUSIC :	SEMPRE, BELL, NATURAL, FERMATA
WATER :	WETLAND, CHANNEL, CHANNEL, THIRST

Puzzle #154

CONNECTION :	AFFILIATION, HOOKUP, COMMUNICATION, ATTACHMENT
EFFULGENT :	FLAMBOYANT, GLARE, DAZZLING, GLITTERING
FOOD :	SNACK, TURNIP, CUPBOARD, COOK
COMPUTERS :	FOLDER, HTML, LINK, MIRROR

Puzzle #155

JOURNEY :	TREK, ROAMING, DISCOVERY, TRAVEL
COMPUTERS :	SCAN, CD, DRAG, PORTAL
OBFUSCATE :	CAMOUFLAGE, CLOAK, EQUANIMITY, XENOPHOBIA
EPHEMERAL :	LAPSE, EPHEMERAL, FICKLE, EPHEMERAL

Puzzle #156

NAME :	WORD, SURNAME, MONIKER, DESIGNATION
TRANSPORT :	PETROL, CRUISE, ULTIMATE, MERCEDES
WATER :	MARSH, TRIBUTARY, ESTUARY, SWAMP
ELEVATION :	ACCLIMATIZATION, ESCARPMENT, LOW, PROMINENCE

Puzzle #157

LOVE :	ATTACHMENT, HEART, DESIRE, LOVE
ANIMALS :	COBRA, FIREANT, ISOPOD, PANGOLIN
OBJECT'S PHYSICAL SIZE :	LEAN, BULKY, DELICATE, ENORMOUS
TECHNOLOGY :	CODING, CYBERNETICS, ROBOTICS, CLOUD COMPUTING

Puzzle #158

WEATHER :	SUNSHINE, BREEZE, OVERCAST, HYDROLOGY
MAMMALS :	FOX, LEOPARD, ELEPHANT, GIRAFFE
EFFULGENT :	VIVID, EFFERVESCENT, RADIANCE, PHOSPHORESCENT
MUSICAL INSTRUMENTS :	BONGO, SYNTHESIZER, FLUTE, BAGPIPES

Puzzle #159

OBJECT'S PHYSICAL SIZE :	SLENDER, COLOSSAL, LANKY, GIANT
NAME :	NAME, LEGACY, HONORARY, IDENTITY
AMERICAN FOOTBALL :	INTERCEPTION, DEFENSIVE LINE, SAFETY, EXTRA POINT
BODY :	THORAX, PHALANGES, ESOPHAGUS, ULNA

Puzzle #160

DREAM :	DREAM, DREAMLAND, DREAMCATCHER, UTOPIA
MUSIC :	PESANTE, BASS, OVERTONE, VIOLIN
SOLAR SYSTEM :	RHEA, CHARON, SINOPE, EUROPA
COUNTRIES :	SINGAPORE, CHINA, SYRIA, AUSTRALIA

Puzzle #161

ASTRONOMY :	DUST, CLUSTER, EQUINOX, HYDROGEN
EFFULGENT :	ELATED, LAMBENT, BEAMING, SPLENDID
SWIMMING :	BUOY, BACKSTROKE, SWIM CAP, POOL
COMPUTERS :	SCAN, CD, DRAG, PORTAL

Puzzle #162

WATER :	SEA, GULF, OCEAN, WETLAND
SPORTS :	SCULL, SKATE, ARENA, BATON
TRANSPORT :	BICYCLE, MOTORCYCLE, UPGRADED, ASTONISHING
ANIMALS :	SQUIRREL, BIVALVE, OSTRICH, COW

Puzzle #163

SPORTS :	PACK, GAMESOME, BATTER, PICKLEBALL
CAPITAL :	KINSHASA, MANAGUA, BRUSSELS, NGERULMUD
ADVENTURE :	EXPERIENCE, DISCOVERY, EXPEDITION, QUEST
ANIMALS :	CHICKADEE, MEERKAT, DROMEDARY, CHAMELEON

Puzzle #164

FAMOUS LANDMARKS :	TOWER BRIDGE, ANGKOR WAT, PARTHENON, ALHAMBRA
ANIMALS :	WOODCHUCK, DONKEY, EAGLE, ANIMAL
BODY :	CAPILLARY, ARM, FOREHEAD, FEMUR
FOOD :	MARMALADE, BARBECUE, FOOD, BLAND

Puzzle #165

BODY :	ABDOMEN, EYE, WAIST, KIDNEY
COMPUTERS :	COMMAND, DOMAIN, SCRIPT, SCREEN
COMEDY :	BUFFOONERY, PUNS, WITTY, SARCASM
ANIMALS :	TARANTULA, CROCODILE, BEAVER, NANDU

Puzzle #166

PIZZA :	SLICE, SIZZLE, ANCHOVIES, CHEESE
CAPITAL :	NASSAU, YAREN DISTRICT, BANGUI, PANAMA CITY
SPORTS :	SPORT, DISPORT, JUDO, PRACTICE
NATURE :	WILDLIFE, GLACIERS, ECOSYSTEM, MARSH

Puzzle #167

WEATHER :	LOW, INVERSION, RAINBOW, SNOWSTORM
LOVE :	INFATUATION, FEELING, COURTSHIP, CONNECTION
CLOTHING :	PANTYHOSE, BONNET, JUMPSUIT, SOCK
LITERARY :	SETTING, STREAM OF CONSCIOUSNESS, NARRATOR, SYMBOLISM

Puzzle #168

CLOTHING :	JUMPER, TUX, DRESS, WAISTCOAT
COUNTRIES :	VENEZUELA, INDIA, TURKEY, TUVALU
BODY :	TORSO, TONSILS, WRIST, TOE
FOOD :	SHERBET, CUPCAKE, KOHLRABI, LUNCHMEAT

Puzzle #169

PROFESSIONS :	DOCTOR, TEACHER, FIREFIGHTER, ENGINEER
PLANTS :	PEDUNCLE, SOIL, FOREST, SPINE
POSITIVE WORDS :	HONEST, LUCID, ESTEEMED, REWARDING
MYTHICAL CREATURES :	GRIFFIN, UNICORN, DRAGON, PHOENIX

Puzzle #170

SUN :	SUNRAY, SUNKEN, DAYLIGHT, SUNBATHED
HOUSE :	FENCE, TRELLIS, SINK, KITCHEN
ASTRONOMY :	JUPITER, STARLIGHT, METEOROID, REVOLVE
STARS :	METEOR, STARRY-EYED, ORION, CONSTELLATION

Puzzle #171

FOOD :	CHERRY, BURGER, PEPPER, OMELET
OBFUSCATE :	PERNICIOUS, INTRANSIGENT, SESQUIPEDALIAN, CRYPTIC
TRANSPORT :	AWARDS, PROGRESSIVE, ROADS, ZOOM
COMPUTERS :	ENTER, FREEWARE, FIREWALL, INBOX

Puzzle #172

FISH :	DIESEL, EFFICIENT, CRAPPIE, PETROLEUM
SOUNDS ANIMALS :	NEIGHING, ROARING, BLEATING, BRAYING
TRANSPORT :	FUNCTIONAL, TESLA, ERGONOMIC, ACCELERATION
ANIMALS :	MONOTREME, NUMBAT, ERMINE, EARTHWORM

Puzzle #173

VEGETABLES :	BELLPEPPER, CORN, ARUGULA, BUTTERNUTSQUASH
SPORTS :	WORK, POSTSEASON, WOODBALL, JOGGER
OBJECT'S PHYSICAL SIZE :	NARROW, SLIM, MUSCULAR, BRAWNY
ANIMALS :	HUSKY, BAT, GALAGOS, DALMATIAN

Puzzle #174

EPHEMERAL :	RAPID, PASSING, EPHEMERAL, FLEETING
COLORS :	ECRU, APRICOT, VIRIDIAN, LIME
SPORTS :	ENDURO, BASE, OLYMPICS, NETBALL
HOUSE :	LAUNDRY, DOORKNOB, COUNTER, PATIO

Puzzle #175

FOOD :	SPINACH, ENTREE, JAM, PIZZA
SPORTS :	SHORTS, KARATE, AEROBICS, RIOTING
OCEAN :	CORAL, SAILING, SEAFLOOR, OCEAN
SWIMMING :	FREESTYLE, GOGGLES, BREASTSTROKE, LIFEGUARD

Puzzle #176

HOUSE :	HOME, LAMP, BEAM, MIRROR
ANIMALS :	ROBIN, UNGULATES, WHIPPET, PIRANHA
CHEESE :	COTTAGE, CHEESIEST, EMMENTAL, PARMESAN
PARTS OF THE BODY :	THIGHS, CALVES, FEET, TOE

Puzzle #177

SHUTTER :	JPEG, ZOOM, AUTOFOCUS, WIDE-ANGLE
UBIQUITOUS :	PERENNIAL, PERVADING, TOTAL, ALL-AROUND
ENERGY :	PIRANHA, SKATE, RADIANT, TUNNY
FOOD :	ASPIC, BRISKET, SEEDS, RHUBARB

Puzzle #178

COMPUTERS :	WEBSITE, UTILITY, QUEUE, JAVA
WEATHER :	COLD, NORMAL, DRIZZLE, FAIR
COUNTRIES :	SOMALIA, ARMENIA, MOLDOVA, PANAMA
ART :	DESIGN, CREATE, MEDIUM, ARTIST

Puzzle #179

SHAPES :	CIRCLE, SQUARE, TRIANGLE, RECTANGLE
SERENDIPITY :	MEANTIME, UNEXPECTED, CHANCE, SYNCHRONICITY
NIGHT :	NOCTURNE, SHADOWS, MOONLIGHT, TWILIGHT
FISH :	CARP, REFLECT, WATT, BIOMASS

Puzzle #180

GREEN :	SHAMROCK, FERN, CHARTREUSE, LUSH
TOMATO :	KETCHUP, SEEDLESS, LYCOPENE, SALSA
DREAM :	GOAL, ASPIRATION, FANTASY, DREAMED
CHEESE :	CHEESEMONGER, ROQUEFORT, QUESO FRESCO, MONTEREY JACK

Puzzle #181

SPORTS :	SHOW, HEALTH, RACER, SPORTIVE
TOMATO :	KETCHUP, SEEDLESS, LYCOPENE, SALSA
EFFULGENT :	RADIANT, VIVID, SPARKLING, RESPLENDENT
TECHNOLOGY :	NETWORKING, PROGRESS, INTERNET, LAPTOP

Puzzle #182

PAINTING :	VARNISH, WATERCOLOR, PIGMENT, GESSO
MUSIC :	BANJO, FLAT, REED, HELICON
SOLID :	CONCRETE, BRICK, QUARTZ, HEMATITE
FISH :	POWER, ETHANOL, ZEBRAFISH, SWORDFISH

Puzzle #183

TRIANGLE :	OBTUSE, TRIKE, INSTRUMENT, TRIAD
PIZZA :	WHITE PIZZA, OLIVE OIL, FAMILY-SIZED, FETA
CAPITAL :	NUKU'ALOFA, ANDORRA LA VELLA, BUCHAREST, OUAGADOUGOU
SPEED :	FLEET, METEOR, FLEETFOOTED, LIVELY

Puzzle #184

SOLAR SYSTEM :	VENUS, ELARA, PLUTO, CARPO
ANIMALS :	GOOSE, SLUG, PIGEON, ARACHNID
HUMOR :	GAIETY, LAUGH, AMUSEMENT, MERRIMENT
FOOD :	BOWL, WAFER, BURRITO, STEW

Puzzle #185

SKY :	FIRMAMENT, BLUE, AIRSPACE, OVERCAST
LITERARY :	SIMILE, SUSPENSE, HYPERBOLE, PERSONIFICATION
ANIMALS :	MEALWORM, EARWIG, JELLYFISH, GRUB
BRAZIL WON THE WORLD CUP :	2002, 1970, 1962, 1994

Puzzle #186

AMERICAN FOOTBALL :	WIDE RECEIVER, KICKOFF, PUNT, TOUCHDOWN
ELEVATION :	OUTLOOK, PROMONTORY, SUMMIT, TOP
BODY :	URETER, TESTES, EYELASHES, SOLE
SERENDIPITY :	KISMET, COINCIDENTAL, HAPPENSTANCE, PREDESTINATION

Puzzle #187

CLOTHING :	GAITERS, VEIL, JACKET, PANTSUIT
BOOK :	TYPOGRAPHY, LIBRARY, EVENT, PRINT
ANIMALS :	BUTTERFLY, HYRAX, BULLDOG, SEAHORSE
CONNECTION :	INTERDEPENDENCE, RAPPORT, LINK, INTERLOCK

Puzzle #188

LANGUAGES :	PUNJABI, ASSAMESE, TSONGA, KYRGYZ
EFFULGENT :	GLOWING, RESPLENDISH, ABLAZE, INCANDESCENCE
SWIMMING :	FREESTYLE, GOGGLES, BREASTSTROKE, LIFEGUARD
POSITIVE WORDS :	FORTUNATE, LEGENDARY, GORGEOUS, PLENTIFUL

Puzzle #189

TRANSPORT :	VINTAGE, TRAIN, HOOD, ADVENTURE
RED :	FIRETRUCK, RASPBERRY, CRIMSON, FLAG
PLANTS :	GARDEN, POLLEN, LEAF, OVARY
TRIANGLE :	PENROSE, TRIFECTA, TRIGONOMETRY, MUSICAL

Puzzle #190

PARACHUTE :	JUMP, ALTITUDE, CHUTE, WINDSOCK
ASTRONOMY :	MAGNITUDE, BOLOMETER, APOGEE, PHASE
UBIQUITOUS :	INESCAPABLE, ALL-PERMEATING, IMMANENT, EVERLASTING
CALENDAR :	FEBRUARY, APRIL, INDEPENDENCEDAY, THANKSGIVING

Puzzle #191

DRAWING INSTRUMENTS :	WAXCRAYON, BALLPOINT PEN, WHITE CHARCOAL, MARKER
CAPITAL :	NUKU'ALOFA, ANDORRA LA VELLA, BUCHAREST, OUAGADOUGOU
EFFERVESCENT :	FROLICSOME, BRISK, SCINTILLATING, JOYOUS
TRANSPORTATION :	PARAGLIDER, BICYCLE, SCOOTER, KAYAK

Puzzle #192

HOUSE :	STAIRCASE, CUPBOARD, CEILING, CARPORT
MUSIC :	TABLA, UKULELE, CORNET, TRILL
SOLID :	CONCRETE, BRICK, QUARTZ, HEMATITE
DREAM :	NIGHTMARE, FANTASIA, DREAMINESS, DREAMSCAPE

Puzzle #193

PRINTED MATERIALS :	HARDCOVER, CATALOG, ANTHOLOGY, MONOGRAPH
COMPUTERS :	PASSWORD, DELETE, PIRACY, BIT
SPORTS :	HOCKEY, BOWLER, WATER, SUPERCROSS
FISH :	CARP, REFLECT, WATT, BIOMASS

Puzzle #194

SPORTS :	TRASHSPORT, BUSINESS, JOCOSITY, ACTION
ANIMALS :	MONOTREME, NUMBAT, ERMINE, EARTHWORM
CITRUS FRUITS :	SWEET LIME, YUZU, POMELO, KHASIPAPEDA
CHEESE :	CHEESEMONGER, ROQUEFORT, QUESO FRESCO, MONTEREY JACK

Puzzle #195

WHEELS :	SCOOTY, HOVERCRAFT, SEGWAY, AIRPLANE
SKY :	SOLAR SYSTEM, STARS, ALTITUDE, NIGHT
FOOD :	MARMALADE, BARBECUE, FOOD, BLAND
JUMP :	BOUNCE, DOWNWARDS, SKYDIVING, KANGAROO

Puzzle #196

ENERGY :	DOGFISH, RAY, ALTERNATING, HERRING
WATER :	SOUND, GLACIER, CREEK, STREAM
BLACK :	MONOCHROME, NOIR, TUXEDO, PANTHER
TRANSPORT :	SPEEDING, UNPARALLELED, MODEL, FORD

Puzzle #197

SPORTS :	ROLLICK, STREET, PLAYERS, VENUE
FOOD :	WASABI, PIZZA, TEA, BATTER
TRIANGLE :	TRIVIAL, CONGRUENT, TRIASSIC, TOBLERONE
STAGE :	THEATRICAL LIGHTING, APPLAUSE, PROPS, ACTOR

Puzzle #198

SPEED :	FAST, QUICK, EXPRESS, RUSH
CLOTHING :	ATTIRE, LINGERIE, GARMENT, ANORAK
ASTRONOMY :	SPECTRUM, COSMOLOGY, PENUMBRA, DENEB
CHEESE :	BURRATA, WENSLEYDALE, COLBY, CHEESECAKE

Puzzle #199

COUNTRIES :	TUNISIA, JORDAN, UKRAINE, TONGA
BODY :	IRIS, FIBULA, HEAD, MOLAR
ASTRONOMY :	FLYBY, UMBRA, SUPERNOVA, HYPERNOVA
CHEESE :	COTTAGE, CHEESIEST, EMMENTAL, PARMESAN

Puzzle #200

MUSIC :	BOW, HARMONICS, VUVUZELA, ANDANTINO
CLOTHING :	HELMET, TUTU, GARTERS, WIG
HOUSE :	GARDEN, DOORWAY, GABLE, LIGHT
HUMOR :	COMEDY, SNIGGER, TEEHEE, GLEE